S0-EIA-694

*HANDEL AT WORK*

VIEW OF HANDEL'S MONUMENT IN WESTMINSTER ABBEY

# *HANDEL AT WORK*

## *BY JOHN TOBIN*



*ST. MARTIN'S PRESS · New York*

Published in Great Britain by Cassell & Company Ltd 1964
Library of Congress Catalog Card No. 63-13671
First published in United States 1964

Printed in Great Britain by Lowe & Brydone (Printers) Ltd., London

F. 1163

*To My Wife*

*Handel's first, second and third thoughts as disclosed in his many alterations in the Autograph Manuscripts of* Messiah.

# *ERRATA*

| | |
|---|---|
| *Preface, page ii:* | Transpose the two lines beginning 'In the case of the Tenor clef' and 'In the case of the Alto clef' |
| *Page 44:* | 'Into the violently questioning' should follow Example 60d |
| *Page 45, line 6 up:* | *For* Ex. 63 *read* Ex. 64 |
| *line 4 up:* | *For* Ex. 65 *read* Ex. 64; *for* Ex. 63 *read* Ex. 64 |
| *Page 66:* | *For* FAALE *read* SAALE |
| *Page 73, line 3:* | *For* bar 82 *read* bars 83 and 84 |
| *Page 74, line 5:* | *For* $d^1$ *read* d |
| *Page 74, line 10:* | *For* third line a *read* third line d |

# *PREFACE*

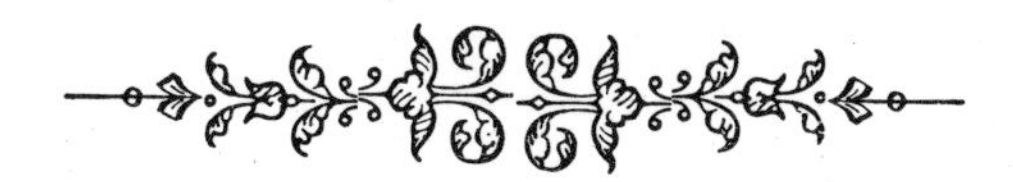

THIS book is a by-product of the greater part of twelve years' close study of Handel manuscripts, autographs and copies with the emphasis on *Messiah*. Although the outcome of detailed research it is not in any sense a critical report—that is matter for another and a different book to appear later. It is written to be read, understood and enjoyed by the musical man-in-the-street who, in addition to an abiding love for *Messiah*, is also possessed of a well-developed bump of curiosity.

The microscopic examination of the Autograph Score and other autograph manuscripts resulting from their collation note for note, word for word with the principal and secondary contemporary manuscripts and the early printed editions, has uncovered Handel's first, second and third thoughts—mostly revealed here for the first time. Thus it has been possible to distinguish between those alterations made immediately and those consequent upon further development; between those purely musical and those dictated by a close consideration of the text; and has disclosed, in the alteration of a single note-value, a melodic shape, a harmonic progression, a word arrangement or syllable distribution, the working of Handel's mind. It has enabled one to sit, as it were, in secret, by his side during the act of composition.

As the evidence consists of photo-facsimiles of the original manuscripts, it is presented, of necessity, in the clefs in common use in Handel's time, but, in general, unfamiliar in these days—even to a majority of those who profess the art of music. However, the following explanation will enable the evidence to be read and understood without difficulty. The clefs concerned are used for the Soprano, Alto and Tenor voices; they are known as C clefs and give the name C to the line to which they are attached. This attachment was shown in various ways by engravers of the period; but Handel hooked the clef on to the line so:

Therefore in the Soprano clef 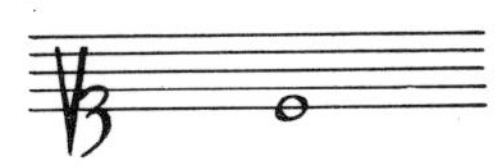 the note on the bottom line is C

In the Alto clef the note on the middle line is C

In the Tenor clef the note on the fourth line is C

Read the notes in all three clefs as though written in the Treble clef but with this difference—in the case of the Soprano clef read two letters below (for c read a);

SOPRANO

in the case of the Tenor clef read one letter below (for b read a);

ALTO

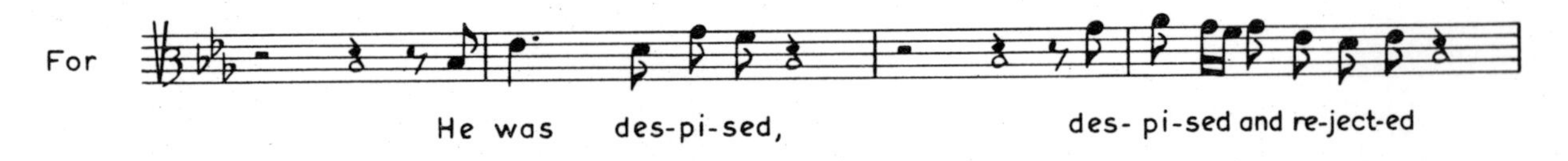

*(sounding an octave lower in the female contralto voice)*

in the case of the Alto clef read one letter above (for b read c).

TENOR

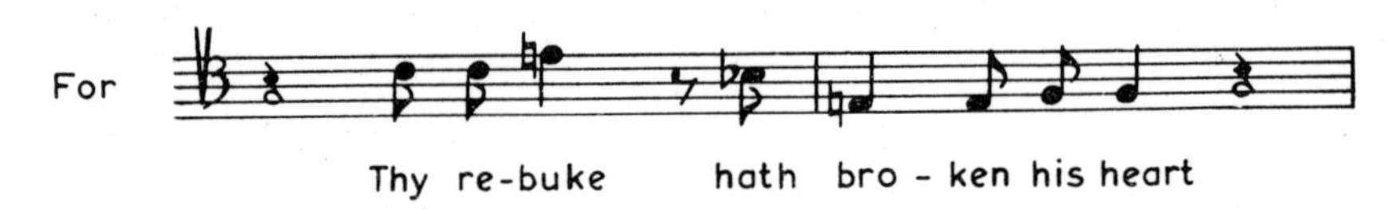

Another point which may need clarification is the part played by the instrumental bass in music of the Baroque period. In this music the bass is of the greatest importance, hence the frequent references to *basso continuo* or just continuo, and figured-bass. These terms refer to the part played by the continuo players—organist and harpsichordist (cembalist)—who improvised a suitable accompaniment consisting of plain harmonies plus countermelodies and more or less rapid passages according to the context. The figures, sometimes under and sometimes over the bass, are a guide to the harmonies the player is to provide.

Here is such a figured bass from a copy of the first printed *Messiah* music, *The Songs in Messiah*, published in 1760.

As there exists some difference in the written descriptions of pitch, here is the description used throughout this book.

All too often statements are made without the production of supporting evidence. In this book, for the most part, the evidence is provided in facsimile photographs of the autograph manuscripts so that the reader may himself see *Handel at Work*.

J.T.

*London* 1963

*Acknowledgements*

The author gratefully acknowledges his considerable indebtedness to the Trustees of the British Museum; to the Warden and Fellows of St Michael's College, Tenbury; to the Director of the Fitzwilliam Museum, Cambridge; the Archbishop Marsh Library, Dublin; and the Staats und Universitäts Bibliothek-Hamburg; to Sir Newman Flower and Mr William C. Smith for their ready permission to study and in many cases to reproduce photographs from the manuscripts in their collections; and to Mr Malcolm Lipkin for drawing so beautifully all the non-autograph music examples.

Also to Mr Robert Elkin and Mr Denis Brearley for their constant help in consultation and discussion during the research; to Mr Denis Brearley for studying the typescript and suggesting many improvements; and finally to Miss Joan Bernard for so disinterestedly sharing the labour of the years of research and of the initial shaping of this book.

J.T.

# *CONTENTS*

# *Inspiration or Craftsmanship?*

INSPIRATION or craftsmanship? First thoughts or second thoughts? The way in which inspiration comes is extremely personal. Some artists, agreeing with Blake that 'First thoughts are best in art, second in other matters', are convinced that they are instruments of a Power outside themselves. Others, disclaiming all 'Inspiration', are equally convinced that ideas come through intense concentration. But whether the idea rises to the surface unsought or only after much patient angling, the flash of intuition that causes the artist to recognise it as the germ from which he can create something of value may well be named inspiration. This first idea often leads to a second—which sometimes displaces the first, as the note-books of many artists of genius prove; so it would seem that, even in art, second thoughts are sometimes best. Nevertheless, the supplanting idea owes its existence to the original one, which, even though it be discarded, remains the seed of its successor. Dostoevsky stated the position fairly when he wrote to his brother: 'Without inspiration one cannot *begin* anything' (the italics are mine).

Even when the act of creation seems to have been inspired throughout—the work written 'at white heat', as it is sometimes said—the result by no means represents virgin thought. Sometimes corrections and alterations are to be seen in the manuscript, sometimes they were destroyed with the rough drafts, sometimes they lay hidden in the brain that made them before committing anything to paper; but made they certainly were.

Schubert read the *Erlkönig* poem a number of times in quick succession, and then composed the music at such speed that the notes 'seemed to tumble over one another'. But who can say that his craftsmanship took no part, once the dramatic feeling of the poem as a whole had lighted the fire?

There have been painters who completed canvases direct from nature, but even one so 'possessed' as Van Gogh recognized the value of a sketch to record an inspiration—to seize upon an idea to be *worked* later into its final shape. Artists working in other media support this conception of work. Even the inspiration that sets craftsmanship to work often needs an external impetus, such as perhaps a commission—many masterpieces were commissioned works. It is said of Bach that in order to start the flow of his invention he used to play, from the figured bass, a work by some other composer.

And Stravinsky himself said, in his *Conversations** 'When my main theme has been decided I know on general lines what kind of musical material it will require. I start to look for this material, sometimes playing old masters (to put myself in motion)'. But he would seem to subscribe to both opinions for in his *Expositions and Developments*† he said of *Le Sacre* 'I heard and I wrote what I heard. I am the vessel through which *Le Sacre* passed'.

*Faber, 1959 †Faber 1962

Genius often sets itself a daily task. Horace's advice was 'Nulla dies sine linea'. Keats when writing *Endymion* completed fifty lines a day; Browning wrote systematically for three hours every morning; Beethoven went straight to his worktable at daybreak; Hugo was up by six and at work as soon as he had breakfasted; Flaubert worked patiently every day an equal number of hours. These men were for a great part occupied with their craft and often in great travail. 'Pegasus walks more often than he gallops.'

The part played by craftsmanship is often ignored by the biographers of a genius. Over-anxious to present their subject as endowed with unusual powers, they in fact denigrate him by making him a mere pipe-line, an unthinking conveyor. The artist deserves neither praise nor blame for the ideas that come to him, but only for what he does or fails to do with them. His genius lies in recognising the germ and then transforming it into a work of art. The 'white heat' in which many masterpieces are said to have been completed, ascribed by contemporary and later writers to inspiration, was probably more often the excitement of shaping something recognised as of outstanding quality—an excitement that the ordinary happenings of daily life could not be allowed to interrupt.

In such a state of excitement did Handel compose *Messiah.* The vital impetus was not a deadline for performance, as was so often the case for his operas (for *Messiah* was not performed until seven months after it was completed), but an inner compulsion. Fired by the text he had received from Jennens, he sat down to work and, as the manuscript proves, composed the complete oratorio in 24 days. The first page of the Autograph Score bears in Handel's own writing, in German: 'Begun the 21st of August 1741', and at the end the date of completion, September 14th, 1741. He may, indeed, have given thought to *Messiah* before composing it, although there are relatively few sketches and no carefully prepared studies. (Apart from the question of date the various manuscripts of 'How beautiful are the feet' are too extensive to be regarded as studies.) He did give thought to it *after* the work was composed—indeed at least seven or more years after, for 'But who may abide' as it is sung today was composed expressly for Guadagni, who first came to England in 1748—but *Messiah* as an oratorio was completed in 24 days. He worked with a haste that was near impatience. When corrections were necessary, and they were often necessary, he could not spare the time to make clean alterations. He smudged out a thickly inked minim with his thumb; he dismissed unwanted music with thick ink-strokes; he crossed out notes and wrote other notes over those already crossed out until in some places it is exceedingly difficult to decipher at all; (see music examples Nos. 3, 10, 98, 137.) But study of the Autograph shows that in spite of this haste Handel was particular about the smallest thing that had *musical* significance, changing the direction of a passage while actually writing it, going back to make some material alteration while still at work on the same Air, or having a second thought for the ending of a chorus and then discarding it in favour of his first thought. We know from his statement to his servant: 'I think I did see all Heaven before me and the Great God Himself', that he felt inspired when writing the 'Hallelujah Chorus'. But when in the course of composition he improved a phrase by altering a note here, a time-group there, or the word distribution elsewhere, the incandescence was maintained by his craftsmanship.

**It could not have been otherwise!**

In *Messiah*, Jennens had constructed a libretto worthy of Handel's muse.

After the loving reassurance of the opening 'Comfort Ye'; the joy of the promise of the Saviour; the poignancy of the Passion music; the derisory colour of the 'crowd' music; the majesty of the Hallelujah; the confidence in the resurrected Christ; after all this, the joy of redemption in 'Worthy is the Lamb' crowned by the 'Amen Chorus'. It would seem that Handel could not have done otherwise, in the final Amens, than imitate the high Amen of the soprano in bar 151* with the more brilliant timbre of the tenor at the same pitch a bar later.

Ex. 1

But he did. His first thought was:

Ex. 2

Note the many differences, particularly the tenor imitation in bar 152 an octave lower. Note also the original bass line and observe the chord in bar 155 with the root A in the bass. How dull this chord is, when contrasted with his second thought, which has G in the bass! This second choice heightens the tension throughout the following silence and gives greater emotional force to the three final bars.

*'Worthy is the Lamb' and the 'Amen Chorus' are numbered as one chorus, the first bar of the Amen being numbered 72.

Ex. 3

151 152 153 154 155

Whilst we are discussing the 'Amen Chorus', what a magnificent theme the fugue subject is! Encompassed within the space of an octave, it builds up the tension over four bars by a simple series of rising figures and culminates in that exciting syncopation on the upper octave d'. Surely it must have come to Handel 'dropt from Heaven'.

Ex. 4

The Autograph tells us differently:

Ex. 5

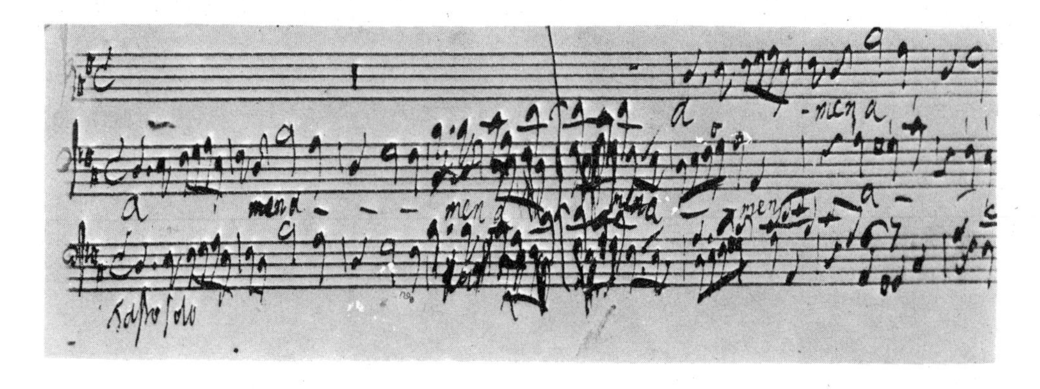

It will be seen that his first thought was:

Ex. 6

This was no *casual* first thought, for an examination of bars 90–91 shows that he began to write the soprano part, bar 90, as an exact answer in the dominant to the subject as he had first conceived it for the bass, bar 75. (See Ex. 7). These bars are very blotched, but it can be seen that the three lower parts were much lower (in some parts a full octave) in order to register with the low-lying soprano part. Obviously he had allowed the first two falling syncopations in bars 73–74 to carry the subject sequentially down to lower B. Discovering the dull finality of the effect of this when he reached bar 90, he clearly then turned back and altered bars 75 and 76.

The 'first thought' (Ex. 6) was so definite that he wrote it both in the vocal and in the continuo bass, as the Autograph shows. It would seem that before going back to alter the bass theme, Handel first toyed with the idea of carrying on with the first thought in soprano at the octave above. Note in Ex. 7 that the soprano minim at the beginning of bar 91 was first a dotted crotchet; the crotchet is crossed out. The second note of the subject (the quaver crossed out) is clearly to be seen.

Ex. 7

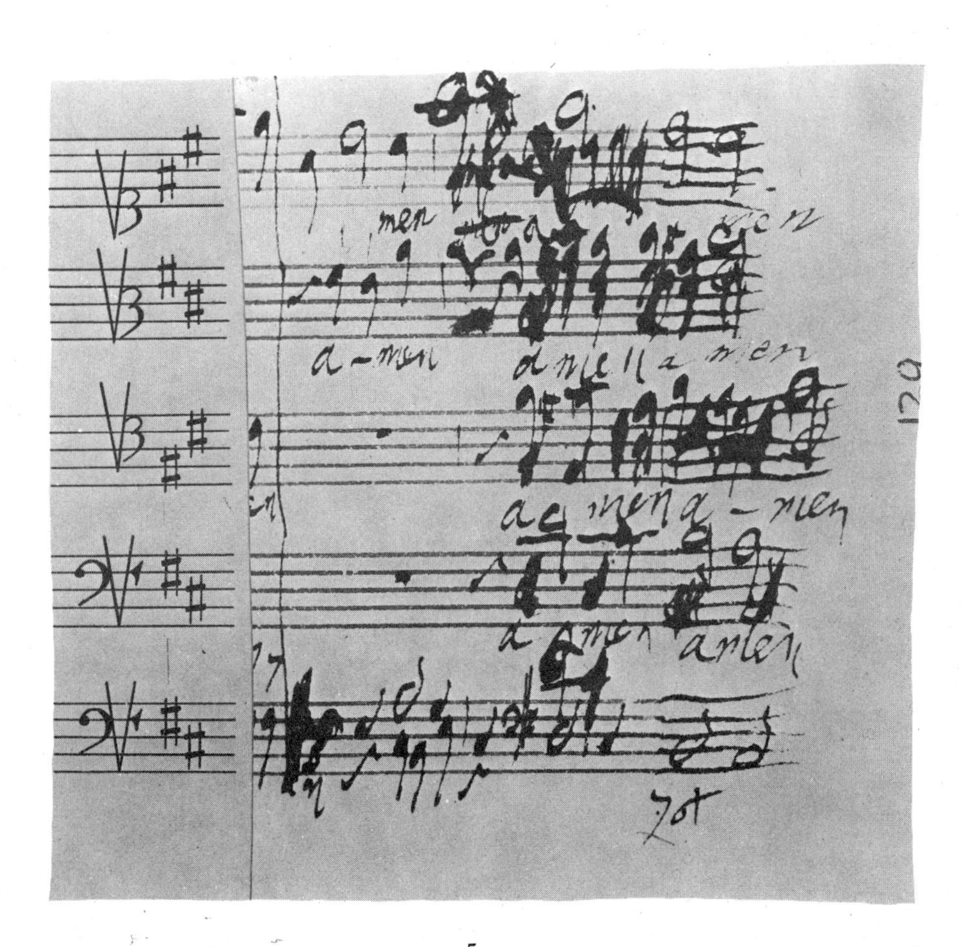



B

Then again, how completely fitting is the orchestral opening to 'Thus saith the Lord'! A forthright and arresting repetition of the same simple time-group over an ascending minor chord, it seems a perfect preparation and setting for the prophecy that follows:

Ex. 8

But this was not Handel's first idea. He first conceived this movement not as an accompanied recitative but as an arioso, with an orchestral introduction based upon the first notes of the voice part. It is pedestrian in the extreme.

Ex. 9

This (Ex. 9) is taken from the clean copy made by Smith in the Dublin Score, from the following bars left by Handel in the Autograph Score:

Ex. 10

In spite of the many alterations, crossings out and overwriting, the original thought can be discerned. He first introduced the voice at bar 4, but then changed the style and at bar 6 wrote the word 'Recit'. After this, he decided to alter the opening, discarded the arioso style, rewrote the first two bars as we now know them, crossed out the word 'Recit'. at bar 6 and rewrote it in the left margin above the vocal stave; and, having crossed through the *a tempo ordinario* and *Grave*—indications of the measured music of aria or arioso—he wrote 'accomp' over the 1st violin stave, to show beyond any doubt the change from arioso to recitativo accompagnato.

Handel must have made these alterations some time after the completion of the score, for this number was copied in the Dublin Score with the original arioso opening. The 'second thought' is on a second half-sheet of manuscript, caught in the binding but hanging loose so that the 'first thought' is also clearly to be seen.

GEORGE FREDERIC HANDEL (FROM THE PAINTING BY THOMAS HUDSON IN POSSESSION OF SIR NEWMAN FLOWER)

Dull is the bass who fails to experience a thrill as he sings the sweeping curve between bars 40 and 41 in 'Lift up your heads'. The descent to the low G, followed by the upward octave leap from c to c' with the succeeding *fioritura**, makes a magnificent vocal gesture to greet the King of Glory:

Ex. 11

But as Handel first thought it the glory was somewhat shorn. This is what he wrote:

Ex. 12

Shorn, and only by so little as a quaver—the last half of beat 4 in bar 40—yet how trite by comparison that shorn beat sounds! How deprived of its glory is the following octave C when unheralded by the falling octave to the low G!

Yet another transformation, effected by a minute alteration, is to be found in the soprano line of the 'Amen Chorus', at bar 104. Beginning at bar 102, the four-part vocal harmony has the 'Amen' subject for its foundation in the bass, and in the soprano part Handel has written a vocal line of great brilliance, consisting of leaping fourths and fifths and octaves.

Ex. 13

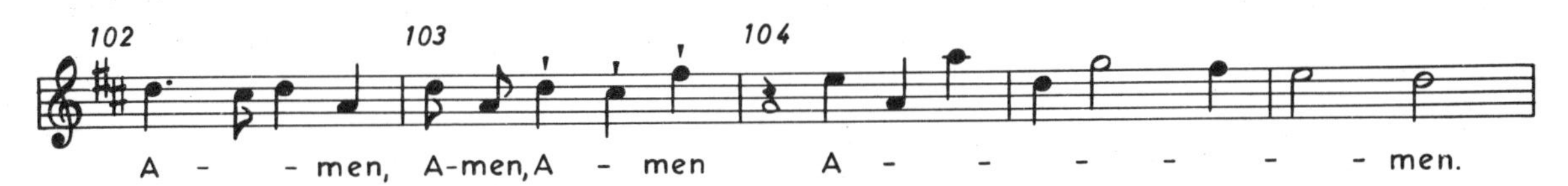


Here is his first thought. Observe the first note in bar 104:

Ex. 14

Those exulting leaps would have lost their brilliance had Handel failed to alter just that one note.

*See footnote page 23.

It is fascinating to watch the mind of such a master craftsman at work. Studying the Autograph, one hears him thinking aloud, rejecting something even as he writes, either because it is not good enough or because it will lead in the wrong direction—much as a poet will reject a word because it entails an awkward rhyme or because the only possible rhyme to come would place the emphasis on the wrong idea. In the middle Alla Breve section of 'But who may abide' Handel conveys the idea of a consuming fire by means of a descending scale, made all the more effective by momentarily turning back upon itself before sweeping down to its conclusion:

Ex. 15

He might have repeated the pattern in bar 132:

Ex. 16

but had he done so he would have anticipated the fourth-beat c', robbed it of the effective approach by leap from the g' above and taken the colour out of the following d' flat. Instead of repeating the pattern he altered it by just two notes:

Ex. 17

A touch of genius—but the touch was nearly missed, for, as the following example from the Autograph manuscript in the Dublin Copy shows—observe, in bar 132, the note-head d'—he was about to repeat the pattern. Having altered the note Handel made clear the alteration by writing the letter f above the note.

Ex. 18

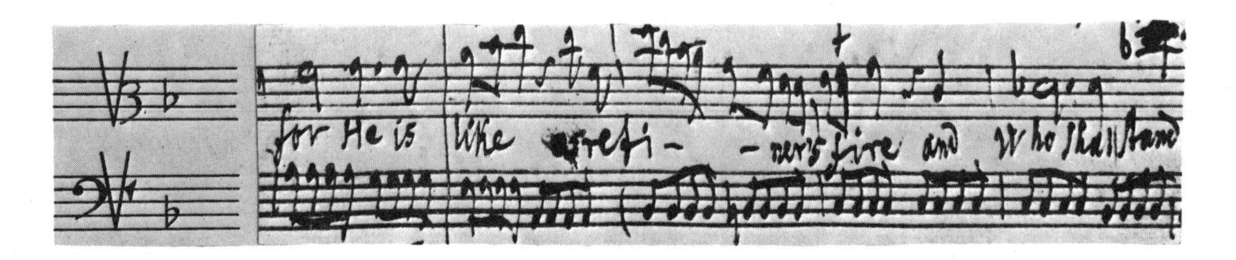

Handel's selection of the exact vocal timbre and register to suit the music to the words seems unerring. Consider the ending of 'All we like sheep'. How befitting is the timbre of the bass voice to the solemn declaration: 'And the Lord hath laid on Him the iniquity of us all'! Again, could any voice but the tenor express so well the call to positive action in the opening of 'Let us break their bonds asunder'? The use at this point of greater forces, say full choir and orchestra, would have been miserably ineffective, whereas Handel's single choral line of tenor timbre starting on the high g'' is thrilling, particularly after the medium *tessitura** of the preceding 'Why do the nations'. Can anyone imagine a voice other than the tenor for the announcement of the fugue subject 'And cast away' in the same chorus?

Ex. 19

Handel could! He first gave it to the bass. And this was no accident, for he also wrote it on the *basso continuo* stave, in the bass clef. Further, he wrote it in two ways, first note for note with the vocal theme and then on a lower stave with the semiquaver runs simplified—for the double bass players of those days were not expected to have the same dexterity as other string players.

Ex. 20

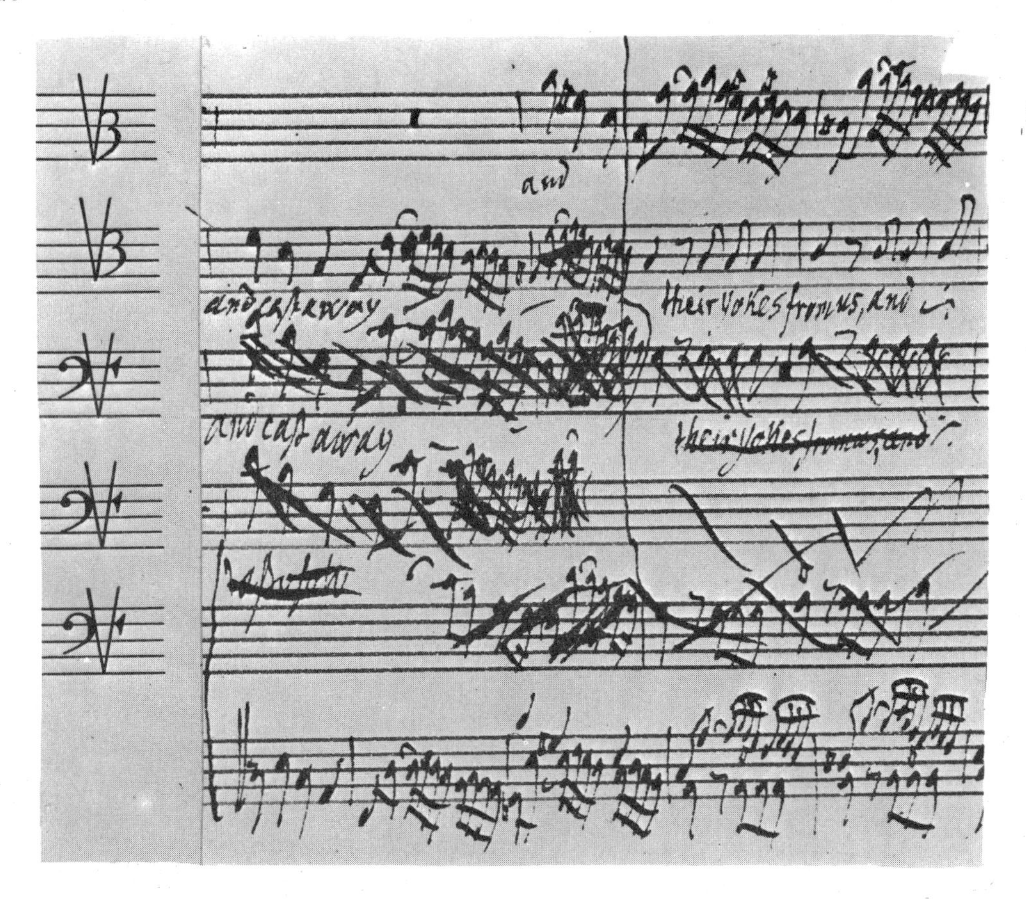


*The 'lie' or average pitch of a melody.

Note also the *basso continuo* part written after the alteration was made and in the alto clef.

The example shows that he had written only three bars before he realised how much better this statement would sound in the more brilliant tenor timbre.

A similar thing happened, but in reverse, in the chorus 'Behold the Lamb of God'. Handel first gave the opening vocal statement of the theme to the soprano imitated at a half bar by the alto. Obviously, however, from the state of the following bars he repented no less immediately and changed the order, so giving the opening statement to the alto.

Ex. 21

The method of performing the sequence 'Since by man came death' has been the subject of much discussion. The first and third numbers have been variously sung as chorus, semi-chorus and quartet, accompanied and unaccompanied. The question of Handel's real intentions here has occupied many minds. But no one has questioned the text itself—the opening minor chord with its low registration, bounded by the soprano on e' and the bass on A, the whole gradually and quietly lifting from the diatonic fore-phrase through the rising chromatic answering phrase to the octave above. How brilliant by contrast is the following chorus with its high *tessitura*.

Ex. 22

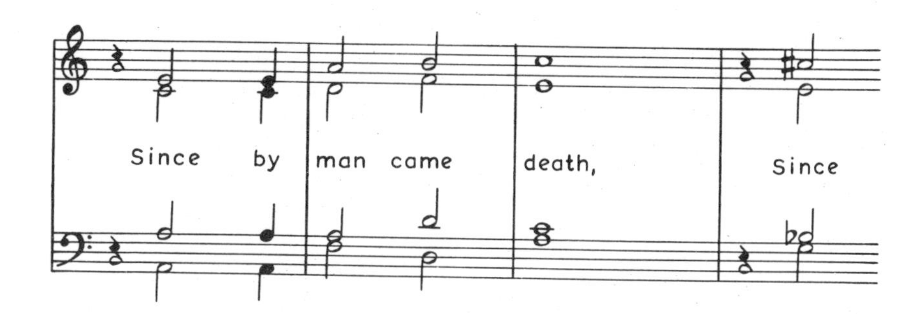


And yet it is clear that for the beginning of the sequence Handel originally wrote:

Ex. 23

Ex. 24

With so high a vocal registration the colour would have been far too bright and the upward progression not possible. Genius nodded for a moment, but craftsmanship came to the rescue.

* * *

A cat sharpens its claws by sharpening its claws! So must the creative artist sit down and put himself to the task of creating. Much of what he produces may be second-rate, but every so often something of first-rate quality will be thrown up. Most of the finest artists have left some works quite unworthy of their genius, and Handel was no exception. Most of his compositions are of great length, and it is not a matter for surprise that somewhere in many of them is to be found second-rate Handel. But not in *Messiah.* Although Handel had dedicated the greater part of his professional life to writing for the theatre: although *Messiah* was composed for the theatre: although all London performances under his direction (apart from those given from 1750 onwards in the Foundling Chapel for the benefit of the Foundling Hospital) took place in a theatre or a tavern: although nothing was further from his mind than to write church music for the edification of the faithful—yet, it would seem that faced with Jennens's libretto he was impelled to do something more than write first-rate entertainment, that he was particularly inspired to make, if only for himself, 'a glorious euphony to the glory of God'. Certain it is that when, in *Messiah,* his pen wrote something less than worthy of his theme he was quick to reject it.

A striking example is to be seen in the first of the Passion choruses. How surely it moves to its conclusion, with nothing to mar the expression of its passionate sorrow!

Ex. 25

Yet what Handel originally wrote was this:

Ex. 26

Observe the rhetorical repetition of 'Behold', and the intrusion of the perfect cadence in B flat major; also the unusual distribution of the parts in the first 'Behold'.

However, from the Autograph it is clear that no sooner was this written than it was discarded.

Ex. 27

There is clear evidence in the Autograph that Handel intended the three choruses 'Surely He hath borne our griefs', 'And with His stripes', and 'All we like sheep have gone astray' to be sung as one, without a break. The final bars of 'Surely' take only half a page of manuscript. They are immediately followed without a double bar or break of any kind by 'And with His stripes', which in turn is without the clefs that indicate the beginning of a new number. The only addition is the sign to indicate the alteration of time—the key is unchanged. The final bars of 'And with His stripes' take a whole page of manuscript, but although 'All we like sheep' begins the following page, it also is without clefs. The most obvious indication, however, is the half-close at the end of 'And with His stripes', the perfect means of indicating continuity. But Handel was not at first so sure about it for he had another thought, and, most amazingly, it was a full close.

Ex. 28

Here it is crossed out in ink:

Ex. 29

From the colour and condition of the ink it is clear that he discarded it at the time of composition—and how right he was!

Quantz wrote 'The tongue must articulate on the wind instruments and the bow on the stringed instruments—the fingers cannot alone produce musical speech; the tongue and the bow must help, and it is these which affect most the expression of a piece.'

No phrase supplies more food for this kind of thought than the melodic line of the opening ritornello to 'O thou that tellest', for, although Handel wrote bowing indications only in bar 91 (couplet slurs) and over the written-out slide in bars 97, 98 and 99, and in four out of the thirteen other repetitions of this figure, it is more than a reasonable assumption that in performance he would not suffer the unrelieved six bars of semiquavers (bars 3 to 8 inclusive) to be played all with separate bows.

Ex. 30

It is not that it is difficult to find an effective bowing. The phrase—leaping from first to fourth string during running semiquaver passages, and on an unaccented part both of beat and bar—is so full of character that it lends itself to all kinds of bowing. The question is not which is the most effective of them, but rather how did Handel think of this phrase? Had he stuck to his first thought, there would not have been any question to answer, since that leaping figure that seems to us such an integral part of 'O thou that tellest' was very nearly a plain descending scale passage from d''' down to f'' sharp as later happened in bar 9. It will be seen from the Ex. 31 that after writing this scale Handel altered the third note, b'', to d''', drew his pen through the last three notes, and completed the passage as we now know it. A slight alteration in itself, and yet it 'made' the whole of the succeeding passage.

Ex. 31

Handel's second thought must have occurred to him almost immediately, for it forms the basis of the succeeding bars, all of which he wrote without alteration.

The Pastoral Symphony—a foil to the sound of voices, a link between 'For unto us a Child is born' and 'There were shepherds', and a preparation for the quiet peace of the first Christmas recitative—coming where Handel placed it, falls upon the ear with complete fitness. Its central episode could not be bettered; it continues the style of the first section, maintains the mood of peacefulness and at the same time lends variety by the transition into A minor (was ever music more tender and loving?), followed by the sequential repetition in G major—surely a sigh of happy contentment! Without this episode the first section would lose much of its colour, for its quiet beauty is greatly enhanced as we sink down from the final G major chord of the episode into the C major of the repeat.

This marvellously wrought episode, however, was an afterthought. Handel first conceived the Symphony as a short prelude to set the mood for the pastoral scene of the first recitative—a mood that was to heighten, by contrast, the growing excitement of the recitatives that follow it. He first wrote only 11 bars; that he intended no more is proved by the Autograph. For, immediately following the eleventh bar, on the remainder of the same staves, he began to write the first recitative, crowding it in by turning the previous four-stave string score into two two-stave scores for solo voice and continuo:

Ex 32.

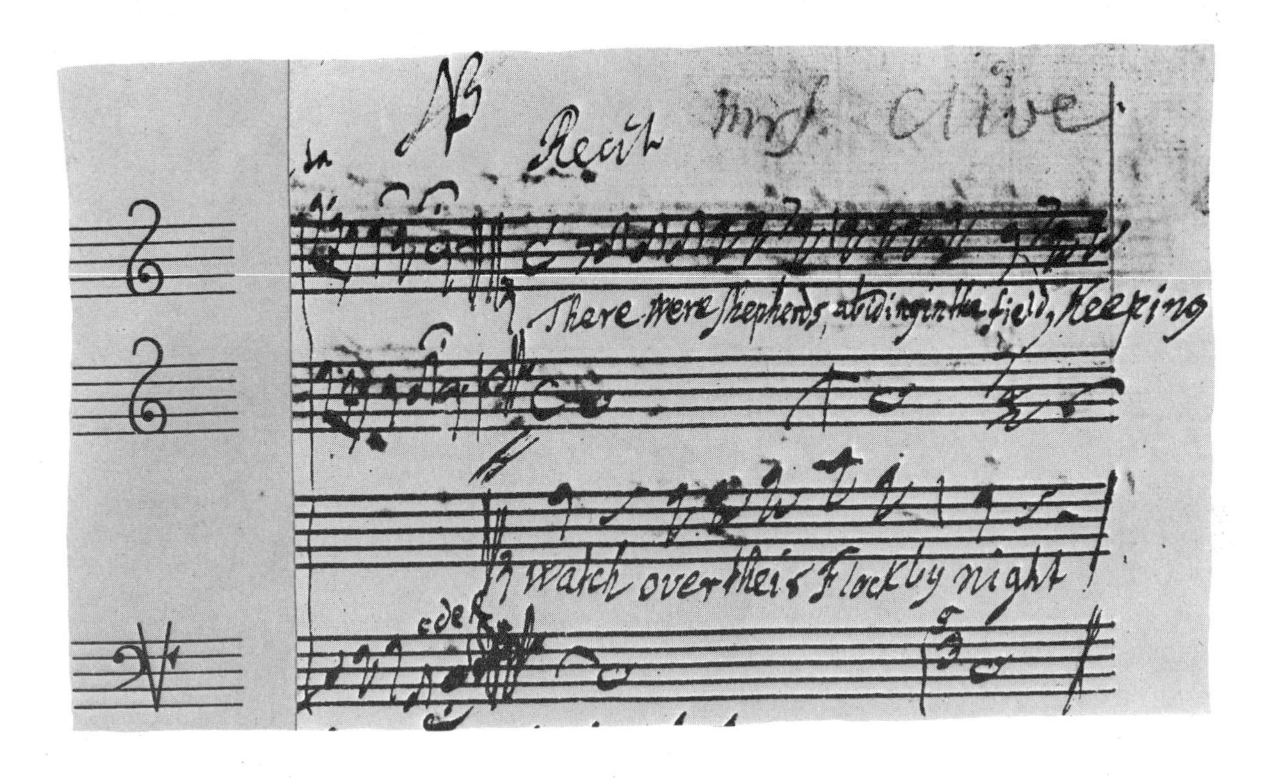


The central episode was written later on a half-sheet of manuscript. It has been said that Handel later deleted it, and there are signs that it was cut in some performances. In the Dublin Score, which contains the earliest copy of the complete Pastoral, the notes that form the link between the first section and the episode (the last three notes of the *basso continuo* in bar 11) are crossed out in the manner of Handel. There is also a faint double bar after the pause note C in bar 11, as well as faint pencil lines that indicate a cut. Chrysander states that the episode was pasted over with paper in the Dublin copy (he worked on this copy at the end of the nineteenth century), but it is not so now, though there are marks consistent with the use of paste. Even so, there is no evidence of the date when the paper was pasted over. The suggestion of a cut is, however, supported by the Schölcher copy in the Staats und Universitäts Bibliothek, Hamburg, and by the copy presented by Smith to the Foundling Society in fulfilment of Handel's own wish expressed in the codicil to his Will. In these copies, both of which were made at a later date than the Dublin Score, the Pastoral Symphony is represented only by the first 11 bars. As against this, the copy made for Handel's friend, the Earl of Granville, contains the Symphony complete with episode and Da Capo.

Further, although it is not generally known, Handel had two attempts at writing the episode—one as we know it, and the other (shown in the following example) written on the reverse of the same half-sheet.

Ex. 33

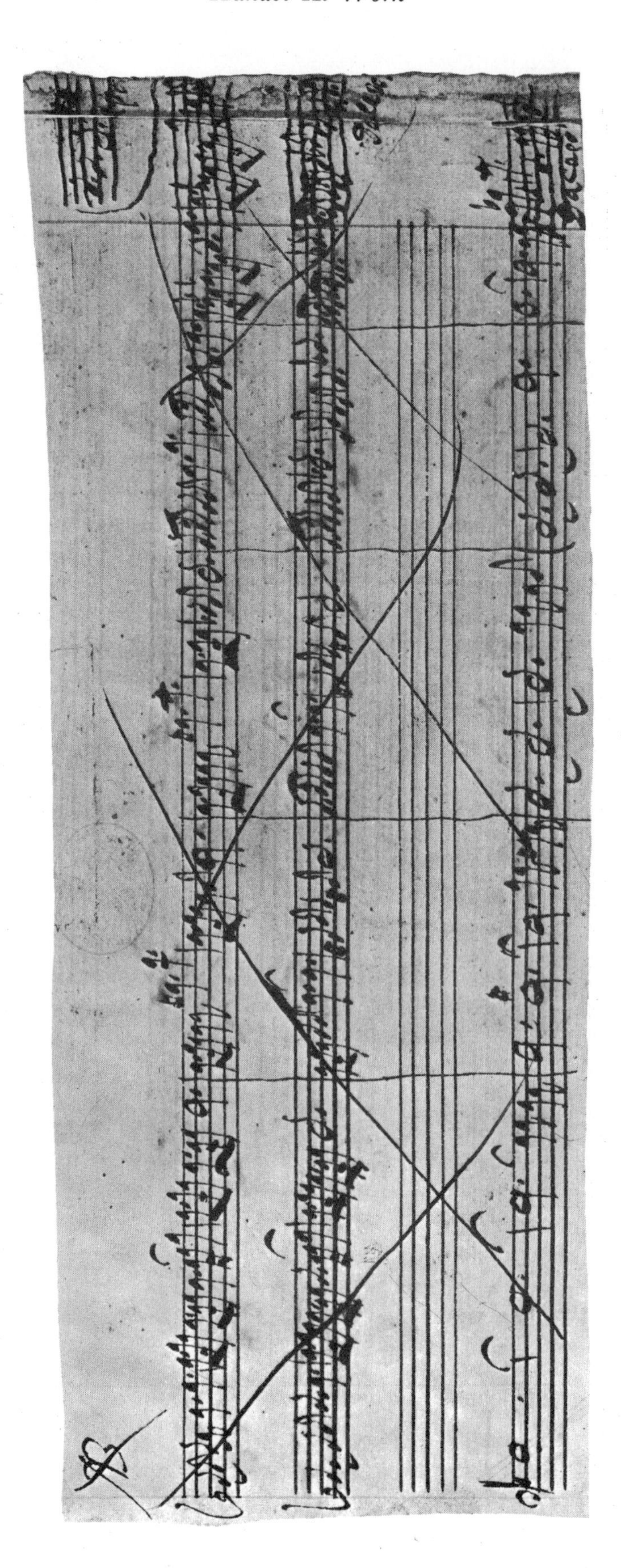

Looking at this second attempt, Handel must have realized that the lovely A minor figure had been spoiled by the G minor ending to the first sequential repetition, and additionally so by the further repetition in F major; and that, approached from the key of F (in which the episode now of necessity ended) the first chord of the repeat had lost much of its sense of peace. He crossed it out in his most forthright manner. He may also have cut his first attempt for a particular performance. But, that he had two attempts at writing an episode, and that he took so much trouble to write a connecting link (see the bass line with letter names over the notes in the pause bar in Ex. 32), are clear indications that he wanted the episode. It is also extremely unlikely that he would permanently discard such lovely music.

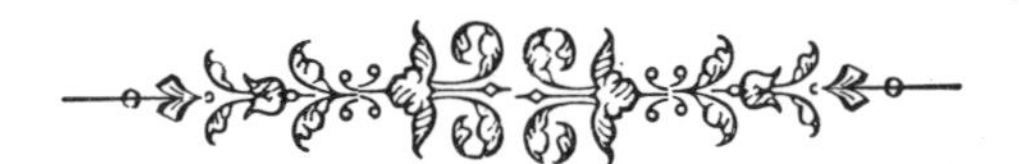

# *Alternative Versions—Which?*

THE score of *Messiah* as published today does not contain all the music that Handel wrote for the oratorio. At different times he wrote more than one version of certain numbers. Some of these seem to have been motivated by his craving for perfection; others were first written to meet the need of a moment, though some of these became the version he preferred. Perhaps a singer of unusual gifts came to town and was suitable for something more brilliant than the existing version, or the available singer was not equal to the difficulties of an Air, or a favoured singer desired an Air instead of a Recitative. The editing of any score therefore involves a certain amount of selection. What one must ask of any editor is that he shall give preference to what the evidence suggests were Handel's own preferences.

'But who may abide' as it appears in the Autograph is not the setting that is sung today. Of the introduction to this first setting, only the first 5 notes are familiar; the remainder of its 13 bars are entirely different both in style and in content. The voice part after the first 5 notes is also, except for 6 bars, different music. Here for example are a few bars of what we sing today:

Ex. 34

And here is what Handel first wrote to these same words in the Autograph Score:

Ex. 35

In the whole of the Air only some 12 bars are alike in the two settings. The most startling difference is that the first setting contains nothing comparable to the later setting's Alla Breve section, in which the all-consuming 'refiner's fire' is so simply and yet so effectively expressed by the descending scales in both the voice and the strings. In the Autograph Score, these words are set in the same $\frac{3}{8}$ time as the rest of the Air; and for the 'refiner's fire' Handel wrote this:

Ex. 36

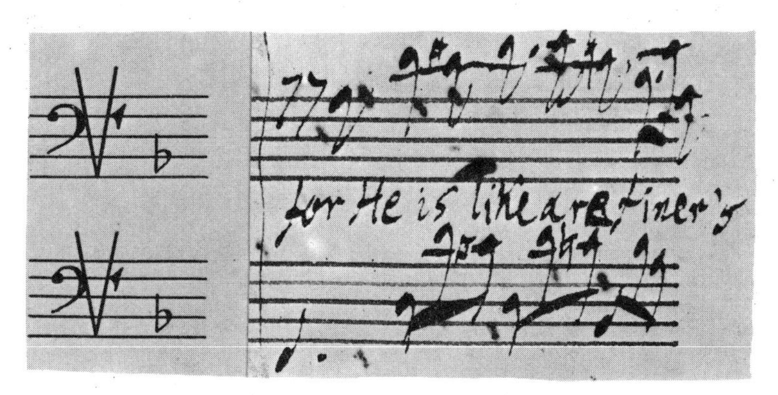

This first setting (composed in 1741) was doubtless sung until 1750, when the Italian male alto Gaetano Guadagni, who came to London in 1748, first sang *Messiah.* It would seem that Handel was so impressed by Guadagni's voice that he reset two of the Airs of *Messiah* for him, one being 'But who may abide'. The first setting was written in the bass clef, but this second one was written in the alto C clef; further, at the top of the score Handel wrote in ink 'For Guadagni'. This setting, later bound in the Dublin Score, is in Handel's own hand. It is interesting that the setting for bass is never sung, and that although the setting for male alto is always sung, it is generally sung by a bass.

We have also to thank Guadagni for causing Handel to set 'Thou art gone up on high' a second time. This setting is practically unknown today. There are in fact three different settings of this Air: one for bass (the only setting in the Autograph Score); one for alto in the Dublin Score, in Handel's own hand and with the words 'For Guadagni' at the head of the page; and one for soprano in the soprano C clef in the so-called 'Smith' Score R.M. 18 b 10 in the British Museum. All three are in the same key, D minor. The bass setting is usually printed and sung (or omitted!) today. The soprano setting, which appears only in the 'Smith' manuscript and the first printed Full Score (Randall and Abell) has the same ritornelli as the bass setting; the first two main vocal phrases begin exactly as in that setting; but the *divisions* are quite different and there is a curious augmentation of the figure 'Thou hast made captivity captive'. Indeed, the differences are so numerous and considerable that this must be regarded as a new setting. It is not known to exist in Handel's autograph.

The Guadagni setting is unquestionably the best. It is without the pedestrian patches of either the bass or the soprano setting, and has a more interesting key-scheme and infinitely more colourful *fioriture** than either of them.

*A number of notes sung to a word or syllable, and generally extending over several bars.

Ex. 37

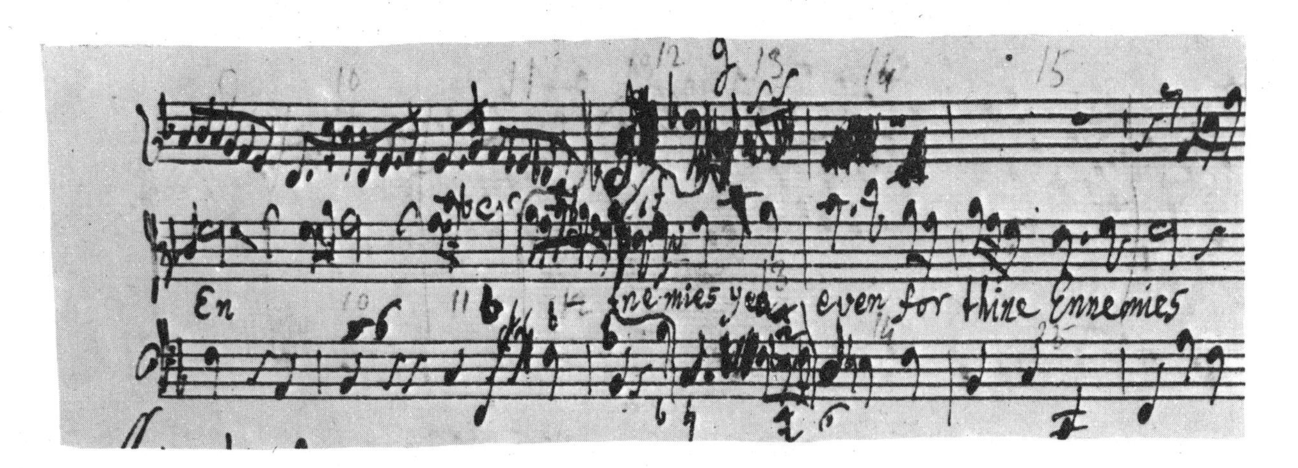


Text books of the period upon the art of figured-bass playing contain numerous warnings to the cembalist against the improvising of countermelodies, passage work, or indeed any music of character while the soloist is singing. This we are told should be done only in the introduction, interludes or coda (the *ritornelli*). The purpose was to enable the soloist's music to make its full effect unhampered by any competing interest. Burney, in the preface to his *Four Sonatas or Duets* (the first music published for two performers on one instrument) warns young players against 'becoming *Principals* when they are only *Subalterns*' saying that 'there is no fault in accompanying so destructive of good melody, taste and expression' as that 'of being heard when they have nothing to say that merits particular attention.' But Handel saw to it that the accompaniment has something of merit to say while the soloist is singing for he often gives the obligato instruments a theme of considerable character against the voice. In the above music example the music played by the obligato instruments in this situation is practically identical with that sung by the soloists in the immediately preceding bars—music of marked character. This is not only an example of composer's craft, it is interesting as an indication of what Handel himself would most likely do at the keyboard when accompanying the voice in those bars in which the obligato instruments are silent.

There is another copy of the Guadagni setting in the Dublin Score, but transposed up into G minor and written in the soprano C clef.

# *ORATORIOS.*

## Theatre Royal, Covent-Garden.

***This present TUESDAY, January* 30, 1816**

Will be performed the Sacred Oratorio of THE

# MESSIAH

**Composed by G. F. HANDEL.**

*To particular parts of which will be introduced the Additional Accompaniments of*

**W. A. MOZART.**

**End of Part II. a *Concerto* on the *Flute* by Mr.*Nicholson*.**

Mifs STEPHENS (by particular defire) will fing, for the firft time, the Recit. *COMFORT YE MY PEOPLE,*' and Air '*EVERY VALLEY*,'—the Grand Scene 'There were fhepherds,'—'Come unto him,'—& 'I know that my Redeemer.'

Mrs. CHILDE 'Rejoice greatly,'—and 'But thou didft not.'

Mafter HARRIS 'How beautiful.' Mafter WILLIAMS 'If God be for us.'

Madame MARCONI 'O thou that telleft,'—'He fhall feed,'—& 'He was defpifed.'

Mr. C. SMITH 'Thus faith the Lord,'—'But who may abide,'—'Why do the nations,'—and 'The trumpet fhall found.'

Mr. TINNEY 'For behold,'—and 'The people that walked in darknefs.'

Mr. T. COOKE 'Behold and fee,'—'Thou fhalt break them,'—and the DUETTO 'O Death! where is thy fting,' with Madame MARCONI.

---

Principal Performers.

Mifs STEPHENS,

Mrs Childe, Mafter Williams, Mafter Harris

And Madame MARCONI,

*(Her firft appearance)*

Mr. T. COOKE,

*(His firft appearance)*

Mr. TINNEY,

Mr Hammond, Mr Norris,

And Mr. C. SMITH.

*(His firft appearance)*

---

*Leader of the Band, Mr. W. Ware—Organ, Mr. S. Wefley*

Violins, Meff Challoner (principal Second,, Bramah, Brown Calkin, Cobham, Chappiel, Evans, Fleifher, Gledhill. Gwillim, Hopkins, Hopkins, jun. Hunter, Ireland, Ireland, jun. T. Leffler, Parnell, Simcock, Smith, Tully, Woodcock, Young.

Violas, Meff. R. G. Afhley, S. Calkin, Howe, Klofe, F. Klofe, Tattnall.

Violoncellos, Meff. C. I. Afhley, Binfield, Piele,

Oboes, Meff. Griefbach, Cornifh, Beale, Dalton

Flutes, Meff. Burch and Simcock

Clarionets, Meff. Hopkins

Baffoons, Meff. Mackintofh and Tully

Double Baffes, Meff. Anfofli, Bond, Skillern, Taylor

Trumpets, Meff. Harper and Wallis

Horns, Meff. C Tully and Briant

Trombones, Meff Rooft, Shœnagan, Drefller

Serbano, Mr Willmfhurft

Double Drums, Mr. Jenkinfon.

The remainder of the Band and the Chorufes

*By the moft approved Performers.*

*The whole under the Direction of Mr.* C. I. ASHLEY.

---

Places for the Boxes to be taken of Mr. BRANDON at the Box-Office, Hart-ftreet, from Ten till Four

Doors to be opened at SIX o'clock,—to begin precifely at SEVEN.—Half Price at NINE.

*The Free Lift of this Theatre does not extend to the Oratorios.*

E. MACLEISH, Printer, 2, Bow-ftreet, Covent-Garden — Vivant Rex et Regina.

REPRODUCTION OF AN ORIGINAL PLAYBILL NOW IN POSSESSION OF MR JOHN TOBIN

It is curious that, in the Randall and Abell Score, the soprano setting referred to on page 23, the least interesting of all and quite unknown today, is printed in the body of the score, while the bass setting is relegated to the Appendix, which is said by the publishers to contain songs 'set after the original performance a second time'. Far from being set 'a second time' and after the original performance, this setting for bass is the one first composed by Handel and forms an integral part of the Autograph Score.

It is still more curious that the Guadagni setting, composed in c1750, was not included in the Randall and Abell Score printed nineteen years later. A possible explanation, other than printing expediency, is that by the time this score was published Handel (and Smith after him) had been using other voices and versions for lack of an outstanding male alto, for Guadagni was out of the country—he left about 1753 and did not return until 1769. There is no reason, other than the important one of timbre, why the Guadagni setting should not be sung today by a bass voice; the compass of the original bass setting and that of the Guadagni setting are identical.

Handel wrote for performance. True, he was exceedingly sensitive to tone colour—and when he originally wrote for a particular timbre that timbre obviously was his preference for performance—but if it was a question of accepting another timbre or having no performance then expediency prevailed. The solo part book used by Signora Passerini in *Messiah* performances in the Chapel of the Foundling Hospital contains the alto setting of 'But who may abide' transposed a fifth higher into A minor; Passerini was a soprano. The Schölcher Score in the Staats und Universitäts Bibliothek, Hamburg, contains a copy of 'He was despised' transposed a fifth higher into B flat major to be sung by a soprano. In the same score, over the first stave of the tenor Arioso 'Comfort ye', is the name of the woman soprano Frasi, in what seems to be Handel's writing.

Expediency—but within limits. There is no evidence that Handel ever thought of transposing 'Rejoice greatly' down a fifth to be sung by a bass! But when he found a bass unable to stand up to the rigours of Handelian *divisions* he did not hesitate to make cuts in his own music. At some time or other he must have had a bass soloist who either was unable to surmount the difficulties of 'Why do the nations' or else had not the staying power. At the end of bar 38 in the Autograph Score, over the 1st violin stave, is a small cross; in the Dublin Score at the same point is a line indicating a cut; at the end of the same score on a single sheet of manuscript is a setting of the words of this cut section ('The Kings of the earth rise up and the Rulers take counsel together against the Lord and against His Anointed') as a recitative. It is in Handel's own hand.

This (Ex. 38) was evidently written for a particular occasion on a single sheet of paper, which contains on the other side, in what appears to be Smith's hand, the final 11 bars of the middle section of an Italian Air. This sheet was later bound in at the end of the third volume of the Dublin Score. So Handel himself reduced 57 bars containing much difficult singing to 7 bars of recitative. The Air is complete in both the Autograph Score and the Dublin Score, the possible cut being merely indicated; but in the later Schölcher and Foundling copies the Air appears only in the truncated form with the recitative ending.

Ex. 38

There was another occasion when the singer was not equal to his task, and this time it was the tenor. In the Dublin Score there are two settings of 'Thou shalt break them with a rod of iron', one the known Air, 74 bars in length, the other a recitative of 4 bars.

Ex. 39

A recitative was substituted for yet another Air—'But who may abide'. It would seem that this recitative was sung at a performance in Dublin, for at the top of the manuscript which forms part of the eighteenth-century manuscript copy of the Score in the Archbishop Marsh Library in Dublin, is written 'If the foregoing song is to be left out, as it was in the performance at Dublin, sing this recitative upon the very same words.'

Ex. 40

'The performance at Dublin' to which this note refers may have been the first performance of the oratorio in 1742 since the word book of that performance describes 'But Who may abide' as 'Recit'.

It is not likely in any of these cases that the recitative was intended as an alternative in order to save time, for what was half an hour or so in those leisurely days? The writing of the 'Thou shalt break them' recitatave is not Handel's, it is Smith's. But the music has the authentic touch of Handel, though it is no substitute for the Air. He doubtless scribbled it on a piece of paper and handed it to Smith to copy.

Chrysander, the German musicologist and editor of the Handel Gesellschaft, omitted the Air from his performing edition of the oratorio. He substituted the recitative setting, but transposed it down a third into D minor for bass voice. The *tessitura* of the original is so low that it could easily be sung by a bass; indeed, in ornamenting his transposed version Chrysander extended the upward range by a third, so that the top note of the original and that of the version transposed for bass are the same; Chrysander's transposition would therefore appear to make little difference. Actually, sung by a bass the loss in colour, because of the change of timbre, is considerable.

It was neither fortuitous nor merely for the sake of variety that, in distributing the Airs for the different voices, Handel gave 'Thou shalt break them' to the tenor. He did so because the words demand the particular timbre of the tenor voice. Handel was extremely selective and extremely sensitive to colour; an examination of even a small part of his output shows how ill-founded is the notion that his orchestration is a sketchy, stodgy, colourless doubling of the choral parts.

Witness the various instructions against the *basso continuo* parts: 'col bassons ma piano'; 'senza bassons'; 'Contra Bassi soli'; 'Contra Bassi e bassons'; 'Senza cembalo'; 'Violoncello col cembalo solo', etc. Observe 'pizzicati', 'col arco', 'sordini' (though Handel died in 1759 and the mute came into general use only at the end of the eighteenth century); and note the combinations such as harp, mandoline and string pizzicato, with divisi celli playing three-part harmony with the contra bass.

He was equally sensitive to vocal registration and timbre (see bars 89–91 of the Amen Chorus, Ex. 7 of this book, and bars 10–15 of 'Let us break their bonds asunder', Ex. 20). And therefore any alterations of this kind, including those he himself made under pressure of temporary necessity, are generally for the worse.

On another occasion he turned a recitative into an Air. In the Autograph Score, as it is now bound, on a page immediately following the recitative 'And lo, the Angel of the Lord came upon them', is a setting of the same words (although Handel here wrote in error 'But lo') as an Arioso. It appears to form part of the original score, and so at first I was inclined to the belief that Handel was dissatisfied with the recitative and immediately set about writing something better. But better it is not! Nor did it form part of the original manuscript, for Handel numbered every fourth sheet of the score; and between folio 10 (on which the Pastoral Symphony begins) and folio 11 there are *five* sheets not counting the inserted half-sheet containing the episode of the Pastoral Symphony. On the other hand the recitative is definitely part of the score, for it occurs on the lower half of and completes folio 10, verso. Obviously the Arioso setting was written later on a single sheet and still later bound into the score. It occupies the whole of one side and only 2 out of the 10 staves of the other side, the remaining 8 being left blank. One can only surmise that 'Mrs Clive' wanted something more 'effective' than a recitative—or possibly Handel himself thought that he might get more colour out of the words. For in the Arioso he made much play with 'And they were sore afraid'. He first approached the word 'sore' with a downward leap of a diminished seventh, and then twice repeated 'sore afraid', increasing the sense of disquiet by allowing only a quaver rest and raising the pitch between each repetition:

Ex. 41

and later he gave a *division* to the word 'Glory':

Ex. 42

But the words are overlaid. Nothing could be more fitting than the simple recitative, in which the excitement of what-is-to-come is caught equally simply by the rising arpeggios of the violins. It is difficult to believe that Handel preferred the arioso; but it was this and not the recitative that was printed in the first published music of the oratorio: *Songs in Messiah*, printed by Walsh in 1749*. Again, it is the arioso that is printed in the body of the first printed Full Score, published by Randall and Abell in 1767. The recitative is also printed, but in the Appendix. (See page 26.) This is clearly in error, for the Autograph Score proves conclusively that the recitative came first.

* * *

In setting words to music the composer, though sensitive to their accent and rhythm, is not concerned with creating a musical equivalent to their syllabic pattern. It is quite possible to set the same words in varying measures and to different time-groups and rhythms, the various settings being equally acceptable as a correct expression of the words. What governs the composer's choice is the mood of the poem. And while it is true that every composer of any individuality has uses peculiar to himself, yet it may be generally stated that a particular combination of measure, time-group, rhythmic progression, tempo and degree of loudness is the common property of all composers as the basic expression of a particular mood. Handel, when first setting 'Rejoice

*See William C. Smith's *Concerning Handel* for the evidence of dates of publication.

greatly', selected one such; not the one in $\frac{4}{4}$ time generally associated with this Air, but the following:

Ex. 43

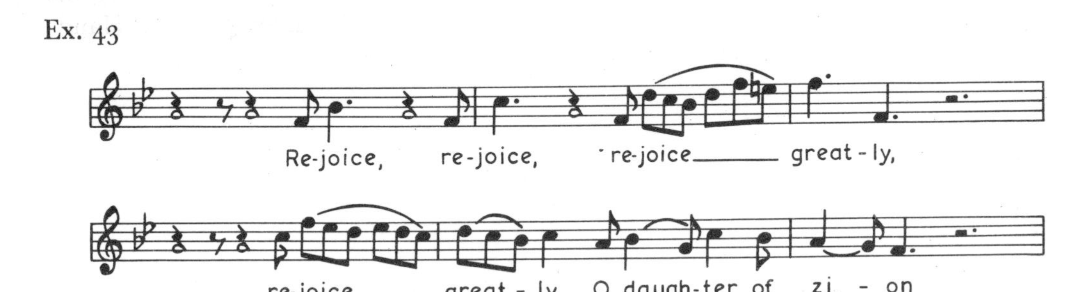


It is probable that, without previous knowledge of the later setting, this first setting in $\frac{12}{8}$, the only setting in the Autograph, would be entirely acceptable, as far, that is, as the middle section 'He is the righteous Saviour'. Here in the middle section, the $\frac{12}{8}$ time-group and the only possible tempo combine to produce a sentimentality completely at variance with the sure prophetic mood of the words—a sentimentality that singers of our own day all too frequently seek to introduce into the equivalent section of the $\frac{4}{4}$ setting by adopting a slower tempo.

Ex. 44

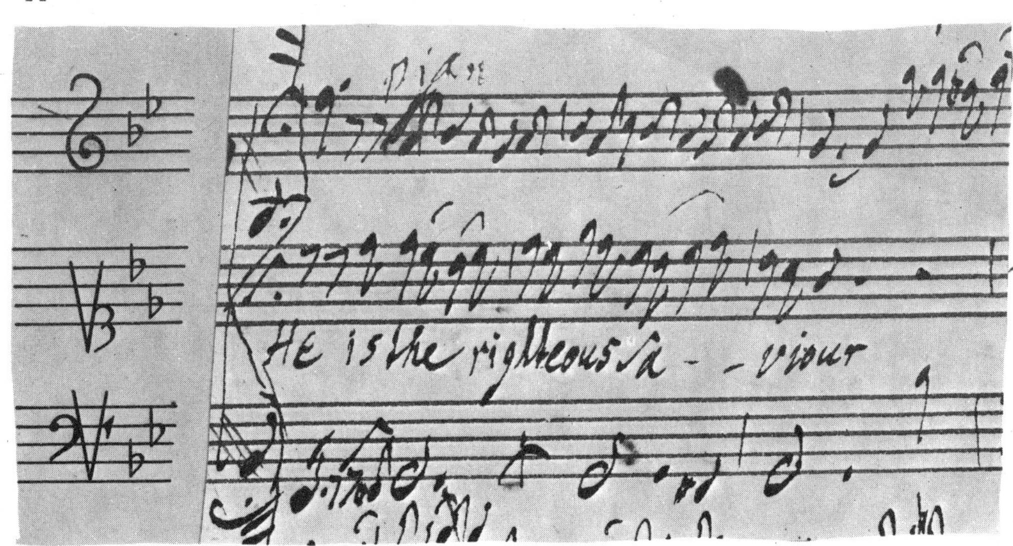


How far the realisation of this caused Handel to think again and reset the whole Air is a fair matter for conjecture. The two settings are essentially identical in melodic outline. Not everyone might agree whether the first section is improved or not by the change to $\frac{4}{4}$, but it is difficult to believe that there could be two opinions regarding the improvement that it effects in the middle section. This $\frac{4}{4}$ setting is not to be found in the Autograph Score, the 'Smith' Score, the Granville Score, not even in *Songs in Messiah*, published about seven years after the first performance of the oratorio; all these contain only the $\frac{12}{8}$ setting. The $\frac{4}{4}$ setting is to be found in Handel's own hand in the Dublin Score; and copied in the Schölcher Score and in the Foundling Score—the Schölcher and the Foundling contain only this setting. It is also to be found in the Appendix to Randall and Abell's Score of 1767—in the body of the Score the $\frac{12}{8}$ version is printed—and the

Appendix to the manuscript score from the Lennard Collection in the Fitzwilliam Museum.

As early manuscript copies and the first printed music contain only the $\frac{12}{8}$ setting, and as the $\frac{4}{4}$ setting appears only in later copies and printed scores, it is possible that the $\frac{12}{8}$ setting was sung at the first performance. The presence of the later $\frac{4}{4}$ setting in Handel's own hand in the Dublin Score is not evidence that it was sung or even composed at the time of the first performance, as there is nothing to show at what date the new manuscript was bound-in with the rest of the Score. For strange things can happen in rebinding, and indeed did happen when the Dublin Score was last rebound. In that score the Air 'How beautiful are the feet' appears to be incomplete, for the last bars are missing. Immediately following the incomplete Air comes the Chorus: 'Their sound is gone out into all lands'; this ends on the front of a page of manuscript the reverse of which is blank. Then follows the page containing the missing bars of the previous Air.

# *The Search for Perfection*

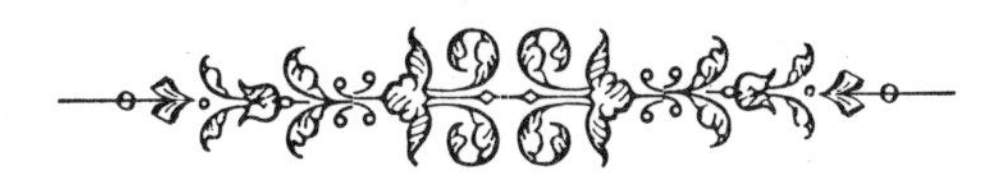

IT is of even greater interest to follow the workings of Handel's mind when, having found a theme that promised well, but being dissatisfied later with the way it turned out, he made a number of full-scale attempts to develop it more worthily. Of this, 'How beautiful are the feet of them that bringeth the Gospel of Peace' is a good example. From it there sprang: a chorus, 'Their sound is gone out into all lands'; an arioso for tenor to the same words; a solo version in C minor, probably for alto; a version for soprano solo and chorus; and two versions for male alto duet and chorus; the last four to the words 'How beautiful'. Further, there is a setting for soprano solo of the words 'The Lord hath given His People the blessing of peace' which bears a strong resemblance to the same germ and uses the same choral idea; significantly, the words here also are concerned with peace.

'How beautiful' as published in most English editions and generally sung today is only part of what Handel wrote in the Autograph Score. When he first set this Air it included the words 'Their sound is gone out into all lands', and these formed the section of contrast to be followed by the repeat of the first part:

Ex. 45

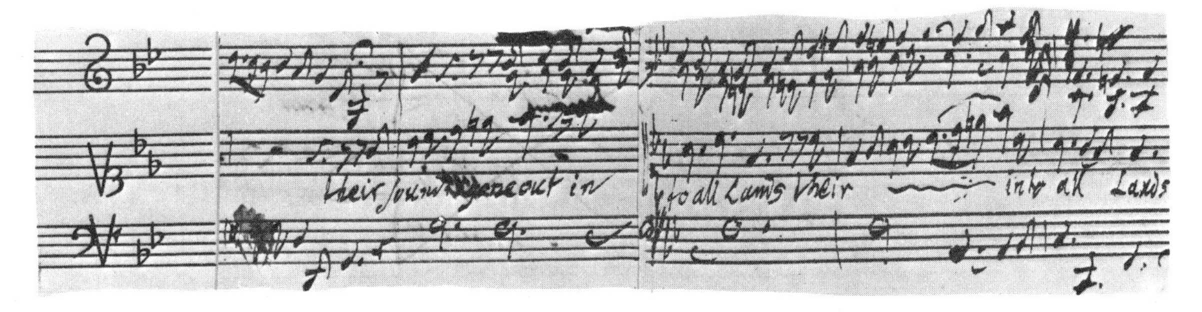


The setting as an Air in C minor (a fifth lower than the original Air in the Autograph Score) omits the section of contrast. Although it bears a general resemblance to the original Air it has many differences, the most striking being a *division* on the word 'glad' in the last bars of the Air. This setting is not in the Autograph Score, the Dublin Score, the 'Smith' Score, the Hamburg Score or the Foundling Score. I have found it in manuscript only in the Score from the Lennard Collection in the Fitzwilliam Museum, and in print in the Randall and Abell Full Score.

It is clear that Handel felt that the words 'Their sound is gone out' (etc.) demanded individual treatment, and that he therefore crossed out the middle section of the original Air and set these words as a separate number for chorus. He did this at some time after the complete oratorio was composed, for the chorus is a separate manuscript bound in at the end of the Autograph Score.

He would seem to have found 'How beautiful' something of a problem, for in a volume of MSS in his own hand (R.M. 20 g 6 in the British Museum) are two different settings for solo voices, chorus and orchestra, one in D major and one in D minor. In both of these the chorus sing additional words: 'Break forth into joy, thy God reigneth'.

The D major setting uses the soprano as soloist. The solo part is quite brilliant, with many *divisions:*

Ex. 46

There are separate oboe parts in the score, rather trumpet-like in style, and an exciting *basso continuo* line in the concluding bars. But although in the last two bars of folio 36 and the first four bars of folio 37 the violin writing is the same exciting reversing octave figure as in the duet version, this setting is based upon completely unfamiliar thematic material:

Ex. 47

The setting has small claim to serious consideration as *Messiah* music. It is not complete in itself, for it ends with a choral half-cadence; evidently something else was to follow. Further, the orchestration is unfinished; the final 18 bars contain nothing in the orchestral staves.

The D minor setting begins with a duet for male altos introduced by an orchestral prelude taken from 'As pants the hart' (H.G. Vol. 34 pp. 207, 239). It would seem to have been composed for the Chapel Royal, as the names of two Chapel Royal male altos, 'Mr.Bayley' and 'Mr. Menz', are written over the solo staves. The Score has separate parts for flute (traverso) and oboe, with strings and continuo. This setting also is incomplete by itself as it ends with an imperfect cadence. It is difficult to visualize a natural Da Capo either in this or the soprano solo and chorus setting.

The remaining attempt in D minor, bears a resemblance to the setting just described. The orchestral introduction, here based on the theme of the well-known soprano Air, is shorter by 24 bars; the choral section, which includes some imitative writing also based on the soprano Air, is longer by 60 bars; and the whole is completed by a perfect cadence. This, like the chorus 'Their sound is gone out', is a separate manuscript in Handel's own hand, bound in at the end of the Autograph Score.

Which of all these settings of 'How beautiful' did Handel prefer? In his search for one that would satisfy him he first crossed out the middle section of the original Air in the Autograph Score and also most thoroughly crossed out the whole of the Air in the Dublin Score. He made three attempts at setting the words for solo voices, each of these ending with a considerable choral section.

It was, moreover, a setting for alto duet and chorus that was sung under Handel's direction at the first performance, not, as generally supposed, the Air; for in the word book of the first performance, printed in Dublin by George Faulkner ('price a British sixpence'), this number includes the words 'Break forth into joy', which are to be found only in the choral settings. Of these it must surely have been the one that ended in a perfect cadence—the one that is to be found at the back of the original score as an additional manuscript. It is not unreasonable to assume that this was also the setting that Handel preferred.

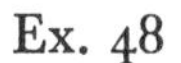

Ex. 48

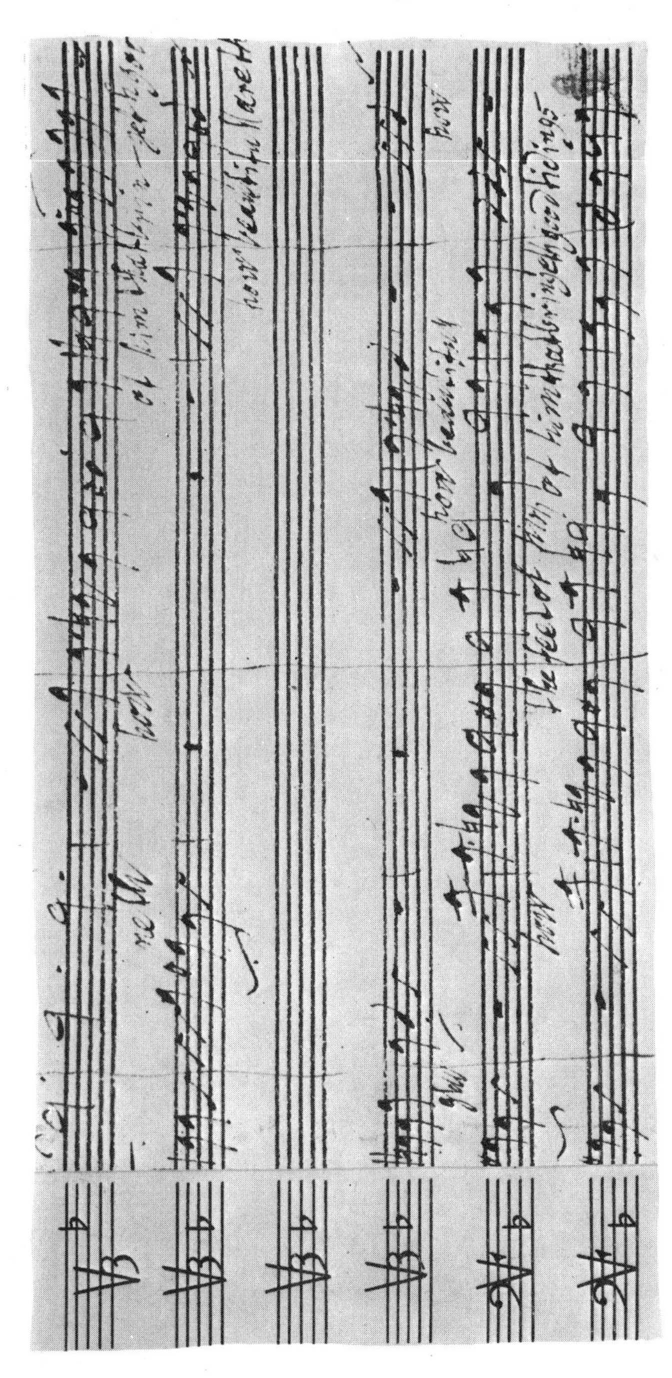

Ex. 49

Chrysander's definitive edition gives a complete duet-and-chorus setting on pages 213–233. But the duet is given for soprano and alto, though Handel clearly indicated in the margin of the manuscript in the Autograph Score that the duet was for two altos. The odd notes for soprano pencilled in the Autograph on the empty choral-soprano stave as a substitute for the second alto solo part (and printed by Chrysander) could only have been a makeshift, as they are a travesty of the original line. Note the inversion of the serenely falling major 3rd of the original opening into a questioning rising minor 6th in Ex. 50 and 51, and the grotesque drop of an octave in the fourth complete bar of Ex. 51.

Ex. 50
The original
2nd alto part

Ex. 51
First pencilled
alteration for
soprano

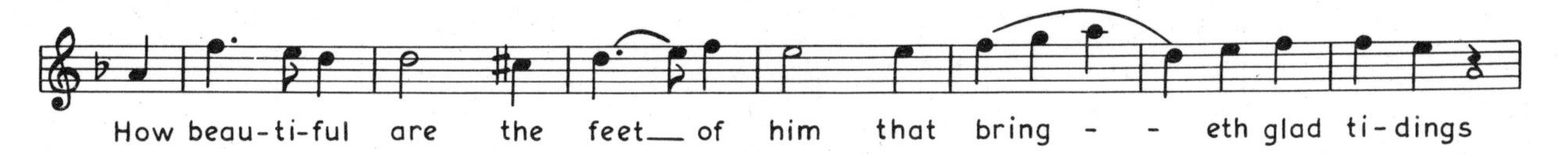


Ex. 52
2nd pencilled
alteration for
soprano

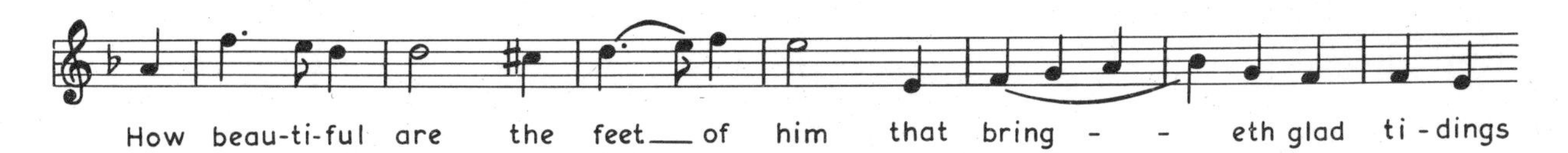


These alterations completely distort the original melodic shape. The opening two notes alone are sufficient proof of this. The whole colour of the phrase is completely changed and spoiled if the opening falling third is replaced by a rising sixth. Sung by a female soprano, at the original written pitch, against a male alto, the tonal balance resulting from the contrast in timbre between the two voices would be a parody of Handel's original intentions. Therefore he pencilled the passage with certain deviations, an octave higher. The first note was one deviation; obviously the soprano could not begin an unaccented syllable of short value on a top a''. The attempt to ease the high *tessitura* by lowering the pitch caused the other deviations; the final solution with the octave drop was a despairing last attempt at a hopeless compromise. One can only suppose that in the absence of two male alto soloists he allowed his desire to include this setting yet again to over-rule his artistic judgement.

Although Chrysander read the proofs of his edition before he died, it was Seiffert who saw the edition through the press. On his own authority he added two pages (pages 224–225) containing the original alto duet. In his Prefatory Note, after describing these pages as being found in the Goldschmidt Score, he writes: 'If Chrysander had not had only sparse notes about G (i.e. the Goldschmidt Score) but could have seen this for himself he would not have left this setting disregarded'.

It is difficult to understand why Chrysander did disregard this setting. He would not have needed to look in the Goldschmidt Score for it; it is there in the duet-and-chorus setting at the end of the Autograph Score, in Handel's own hand.

A word should be said here about the duet-and-chorus version published in Novello's Anthems Series No. 1274, edited by the late Sir Ivor Atkins 'from Chrysander's facsimile of the Autograph of *Messiah* in the King's Library, now in the British Museum'. This is not at all what it purports to be. It is in fact a mixture of two settings. It begins at bar 24 of the Introduction of the Chapel Royal setting; it then jumps to the vocal duet from the setting in the Autograph Score but ignores Handel's original notes in ink for the alto, printing instead the makeshift pencilled notes for soprano. (This is perhaps understandable in view of Chrysander's example, although Handel's original instructions and alto parts in ink are clearly to be seen in the Auto-

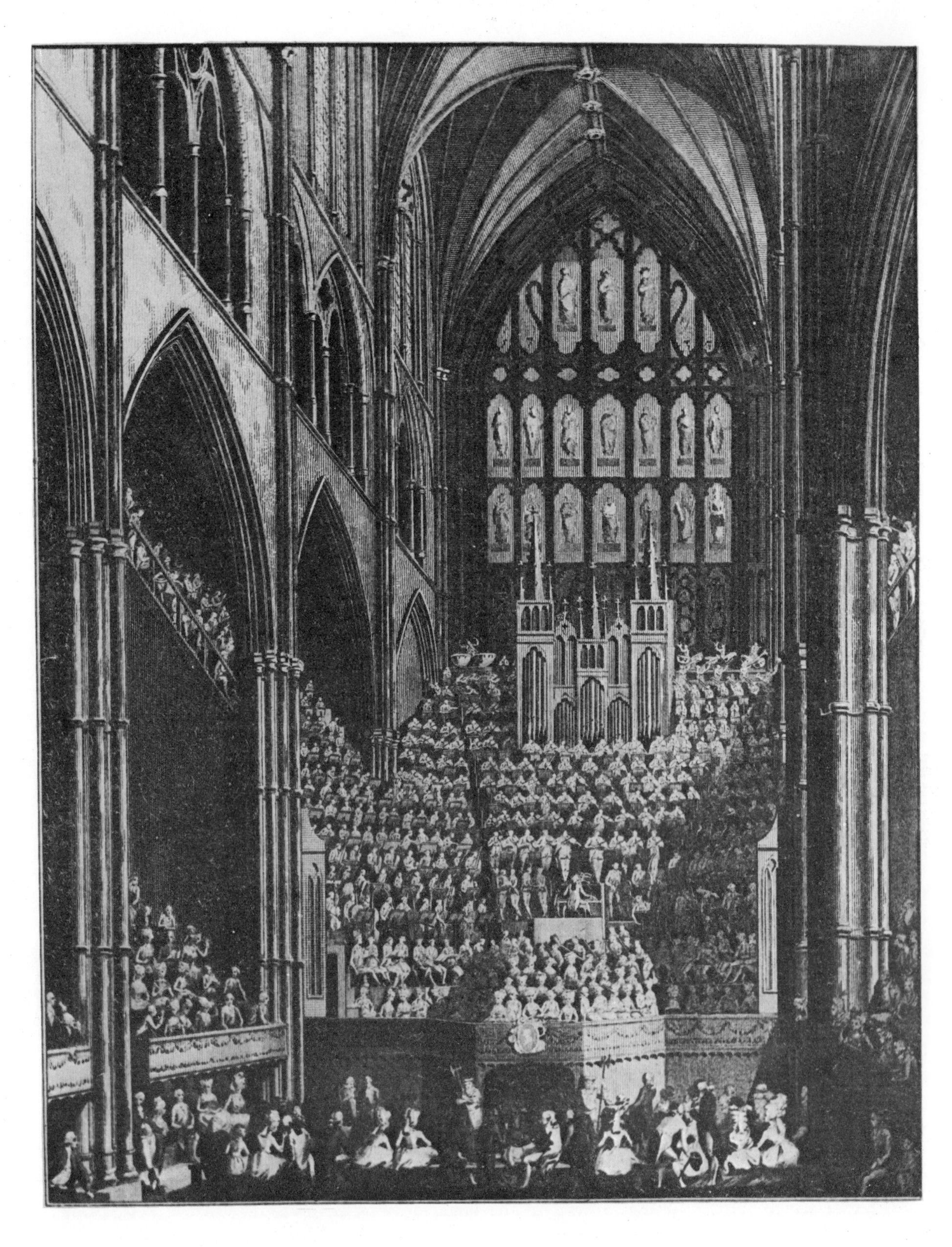

VIEW OF THE ORCHESTRA AND PERFORMERS IN WESTMINSTER ABBEY DURING THE COMMEMORATION OF HANDEL, 1784

graph.) It then jumps back to the Chapel Royal setting for the chorus parts, returning finally to the Autograph Score for the cadential bars. The Chapel Royal setting (R.M. 20 g 6) contains only 62 bars of chorus work against 122 bars in the Autograph Score setting, and, moreover, 62 bars of quite different choral writing. The Ivor Atkins edition is indeed very misleading.

If we accept the D minor setting of 'How beautiful' for alto duet and chorus as the one Handel preferred to be sung, what are we to do about 'Their sound is gone out'? This chorus is in the key of E flat major, only a semitone removed, and it is unlikely that Handel would have used that relationship in this context. Once before in *Messiah* he moved by a step of a second, from E flat major to F minor, when passing from 'He was despised' to 'Surely He hath borne our griefs', but then there was justification in the sudden passionate outburst of 'Surely'! Here there is no outburst, no sense of contrast either way. 'Their sound' is but a continuation of 'How beautiful'. The abrupt transition from D minor to E flat major would be without significance; Handel rarely acted musically so, and certainly not in *Messiah.*

The answer is to be found in the Autograph Score. There, at the end, is a setting of 'Their sound' in form of an Arioso for tenor solo using the same opening motive as the chorus but in the key of F major. True, it is not in Handel's hand but in that of the writer of the Dublin Score—Smith, Handel's amanuensis. However, convinced by the evidence (a) that Handel's preference for 'How beautiful' was the setting in D minor for alto duet and chorus in the Appendix to the Autograph Score, and (b) that the key relationship between this and the E flat major of the chorus 'Their sound is gone out' was not reasonable, early in 1950 I accepted the Arioso in F major as the only acceptable complement to D minor 'How beautiful'.

It was interesting to find support for these conclusions, some twelve months later, in the manuscript room of the British Museum. There, among the Egerton papers, are a number of copies of Handel's scores. According to the catalogue most of these are in the hand of Smith Senior, with the exception of parts of *Saul* and *L'Allegro,* which appear to be the work of one James Hunter, an enthusiastic admirer of Handel. The manuscripts belonged originally to the Earl of Granville, of Calwick Abbey, Staffordshire (1709–1775). In the score of *Messiah* in this collection, the only setting of 'How beautiful' is the one in D minor for alto duet and chorus as in the Autograph Score, and this is followed immediately by "Their sound is gone out'; not the E flat major chorus setting, however, but the Arioso for tenor solo in F major.

Ex. 53

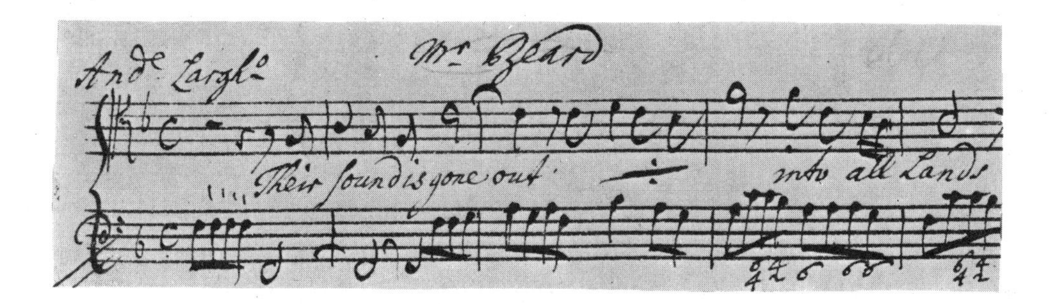


This arioso, although not in Handel's hand has his authority, for in the upper margin he wrote 'Sra Avolio'. In the photographic example this is not to be seen but only 'Mr Beard' in the hand of John Christopher Smith. Smith wrote in ink but Handel wrote in pencil, and the camera failed to record Handel's pencilled annotations.

# *Second Thoughts on Treatment of Text*

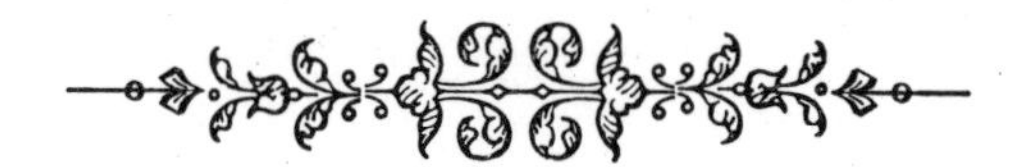

'HANDEL comes with his tremendous power of melody and cosmopolitan outlook, oblivious of all the fine suggestions which the language can offer him, and taking texts from the purest sources of English literature, allies them to music which makes a universal appeal in spite of, one might almost say because of, his obliviousness.'*

It is true that in spite of his long sojourn in England Handel did not lose his German accent and that he remained insensitive to the shape of English words. It is no less true that, like his great compatriot Bach, he put words to music previously composed for words of a quite different character. For example, he first wrote the music of 'All we like sheep' as a *Duetto da Camera* to Italian words concerned with love and beauty; he composed this duet for Princess Caroline a month before he began to compose *Messiah.* Much depends on the viewpoint. If 'All we like sheep' depicts two-legged sinners, it depicts the jolliest sinners one could wish to meet. The dancing *basso continuo* of the opening bars and the joyous rising soprano figure in bar 4 taken *Allegro* make contrition somewhat difficult. But if we regard them as four-legged symbols for two-legged 'wandering sheep', and take them at Handel's own marking of *Allegro Moderato* (*Moderato* being the important word), I suggest that no incongruity need be felt. The lovely 'Slumber Song of the Virgin' in Bach's *Christmas Oratorio* was at first an incitement to revel in the joys of the flesh, sung by Venus in 'The Choice of Hercules'.

Nevertheless, as Colles* admits, Handel was sensitive to the *mood* of words. He did not seek an intimate relation between music and language as such: instead, he sought a combination of time-values which would express the mood of the whole passage. To his insensitiveness to word-shape we owe something greater—his expressive use of what we may call syllabic-rhythm. Rhythm was more important to him, as a means of expressing mood, even than melody or harmony. The force of this rhythm was obtained not merely by means of various arrangements of different note-values, but also through the distribution of syllables. A smooth succession of six quavers in $\frac{3}{4}$ time

would become the less smooth

or the emphatic

**Voice and Verse*, H. C. Colles. (Oxford University Press, 1928.)

or the forceful

according to the number of syllables in the bar and the notes against which they were placed. There is abundant proof that Handel was exceedingly sensitive to this syllabic rhythm. For example in bar 14 of the tenor Air 'Thou shalt break them', he first intended:

Ex. 54

He then realised that by extending the word 'rod' to still another quaver and giving the word 'of' to the last quaver, the mood of the whole passage would gain considerably in strength. Here it is as he wrote and altered it in the Autograph Score:

Ex. 55

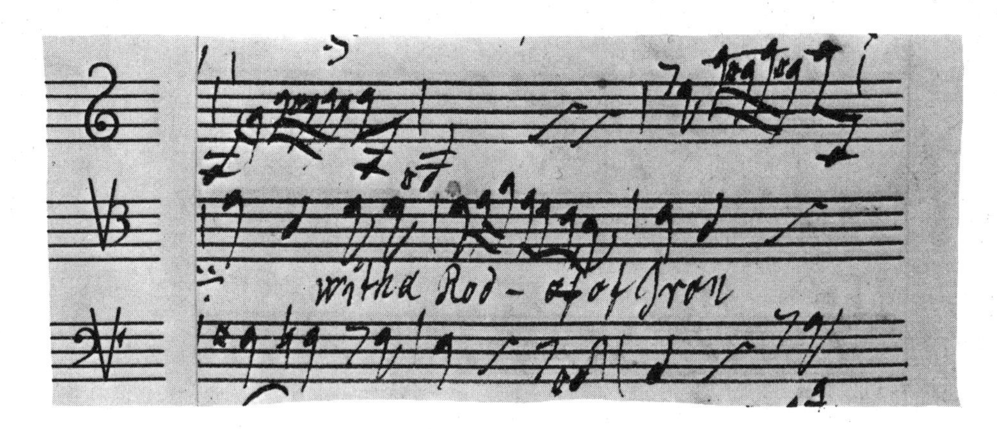

Note the whip-like effect of the word 'of', now that it has only one note and that an unaccented one. It is clear from the above example that he first wrote two even quaver-groups, then thinking better of this connected the two groups by that curving line, crossed through the line joining the last two quavers and added a separate tail for the last note. To remove all doubt, he crossed out the word 'of' and rewrote it where it could be read only as belonging to the last quaver in the bar. The passage as he first wrote it would depend entirely upon the singer's technique of interpretation; for with 'of' sung to the two quavers, the natural effect (whether it be sung loudly or softly) is most urbane. Of itself, it does not sear the spirit. To produce the effect Handel desired, it would be necessary for the singer to accent most strongly each of the two quavers, almost detaching them one from the other. With a slight alteration of word-arrangement, however, Handel puts the exact colour into the music itself. We might well call this syllabic-rhythm 'vocal bowing', for, played on a stringed instrument, *forte*, and bowed in this way, this music would give the emotional colour without the use of words.

When Handel set 'Hallelujah!' to music he set not a word but a shout of joy, so what does it matter that he put the stress by turns on each of the four syllables? He played in a similar manner with the word 'incorruptible'. Here is what he wrote in bars 51-56 of 'The trumpet shall sound'.

Note the stress on '-cor':

Ex. 56

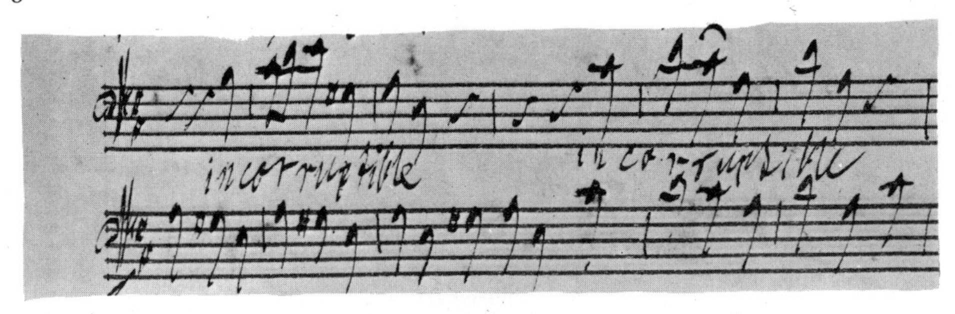


But in bars 36–40 he first wrote it with the stress on 'in-':

Ex. 57

And in the middle section, bars 156 to 158, in setting the words 'this corruptible' (equivalent to 'incorruptible'), he places the stress on '-rup';

Ex. 58

So that now we may say that four of the five syllables have been stressed in turn.

It is fruitful to study bars 37 to 40 of this same Air in the Autograph—to observe his first and second thoughts, to note the alterations in bars 38 and 39, and to appreciate the importance to Handel of syllabic rhythm.

Ex. 59

Examination of this example shows that he first intended the word 'raised' to be sung as one syllable to the six quavers; the slur over the last two notes in bar 38 was inserted later. 'Incorruptible' was to have the stress on the first syllable, with separate quaver notes for the first two syllables—see the separate quaver tails to the first two notes, though the hooks are partly obscured by the thick connecting tail that was added later. Handel then thought again, and decided to break up the one group of six quavers in bar 38 into two, one of four notes and one of two notes; observe the vertical stroke through the connecting quaver beam in bar 38 with which he separated the last two quavers from the preceding four. Then in bar 39, deciding to give the first three notes to one syllable, he drew a slur over them. He completed this alteration by running his pen through the first two syllables of 'incorruptible' written in bar 39 and rewriting them to accord with the new grouping. He did all this, not because of any desire to alter the stress in the word 'incorruptible' from the first to the second syllable (linguistically he would find little to choose between them), but to heighten the emotional tension. The break at the end of the fourth quaver is like a regrouping of forces preparatory to a final attack. After this the two succeeding quavers sweep up to an emphatic *mordent* ornamentation of the note D, followed by the contrast of the three final forceful detached notes which admit of no argument or doubt. He troubled to make the alteration the better to convey the everlasting quality of the Life promised in the prophecy.

During Handel's lifetime and throughout the succeeding two centuries many editors and most singers have endeavoured to improve upon Handel, to correct what they considered to be faults in his setting of English due to his imperfect command of the language. This was far from necessary, for a reference to the Autograph shows that in many of these cases Handel had first written the 'improved' version and later discarded it in his search for a more vital rhythm—one which would the more positively express the thought behind the words.

A very clear example is to be found in 'Why do the nations', the vocal line, bars 36 and 37. Handel's final intention here was:

Ex. 60a

This has been altered and is generally sung as:

Ex. 60b

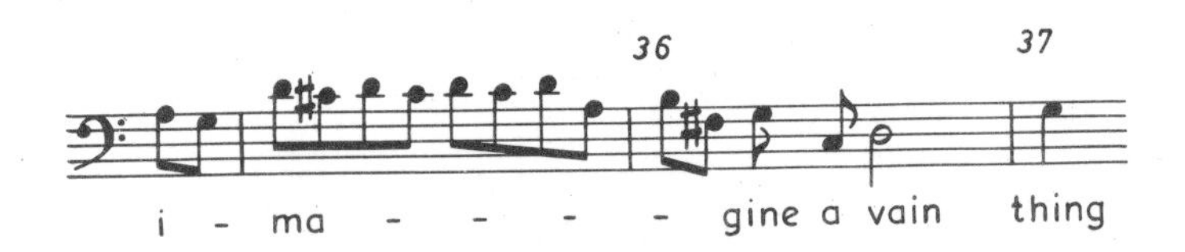


The reason given for this alteration is that for adequate stress the word 'vain' must be given length. The Autograph shows that Handel, at first, thought similarly. So strongly indeed that he set 'vain' not merely to a two-beat note, but spread it over two complete bars finishing with a two-beat note:

Ex. 60c

Then, doubtless sensing the portly stolidity that resulted, he thought again and decided to break the phrase by altering the word arrangement. He altered 'a vain' to 'imagine', broke the group of four quavers in bar 36, beats one and two, by a short vertical stroke across the connecting quaver beam, and added a slur over the third and fourth quavers for the last syllable of 'imagine'. Thus he turned the stolid:

Ex. 60d

into the violently questioning:

Ex. 60e

A remarkable *volte-face* for he reduced 'vain' from thirteen notes extended over eight beats to a single note, only a half-beat in length.

Here is the passage as it appears in the Autograph:

Ex. 61

Note the greater emphasis of Handel's second thought, resulting from the word 'vain' being as it were catapulted suddenly on the last quaver. Obviously this was not a chance result, for even with the altered word-setting he could still have left bar 36 as it appears in Ex. 60c above. That he was at pains to make this final alteration is shown by the added curved extension of the bar line to accommodate the all important quaver.

N.B. The large spread note in bar 36 was first a minim, later filled in ; hence its size and blotched appearance.

'If God be for us', as printed and sung today:

Ex. 62

provides yet another example of Handel's 'vocal bowing' being so altered for the sake of verbal accent that it is robbed of its character. For here is what Handel wrote in the Autograph:

Ex. 63

The sure vigorous tread of Handel's three individually articulated crotchets in bar 26 is ironed-out by the slur (Ex. 63) inserted by another hand over the first two notes. The force of the rhetorical question, which Handel further strengthened by holding up the crotchet movement in bar 27 (Ex. 65), is completely ruined by the substitution of crotchets in Ex. 63. This piece of editing dates from the eighteenth century, for it is found in the 'Smith' scores in the British Museum (R.M. 18 b 10 and R.M. 18 e 2). Although the Dublin Score as it now stands agrees with the 'Smith', it shows in these bars unmistakable signs of having been altered, and moreover with considerable trouble. Here it is:

Ex. 64

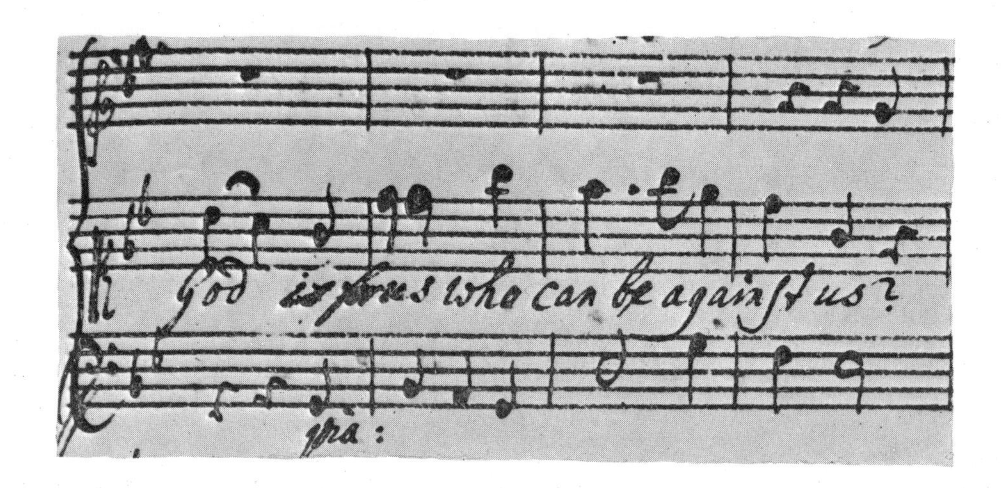


Immediately under the second and third crotchets in bar 26, the paper is roughened where the words first written have been scraped out. The spreading of the ink where the paper surface has been roughened by the previous scraping out and the unequal spacing of the words are further evidence of the alteration.

From its size, the note against 'us' was quite evidently at first a minim, as in the Autograph. The head was afterwards filled in to make it a crotchet because of the altered word distribution, and the additional crotchet (made necessary by the squashed-in 'for') was equally squashed-in between the bar line and the one-time minim. The unequal spacing between the three crotchets is further proof that this first note was a later addition to the bar.

The same thing happened to bars 38 and 39. Here they are as Handel wrote them in the Autograph Score:

Ex. 65a

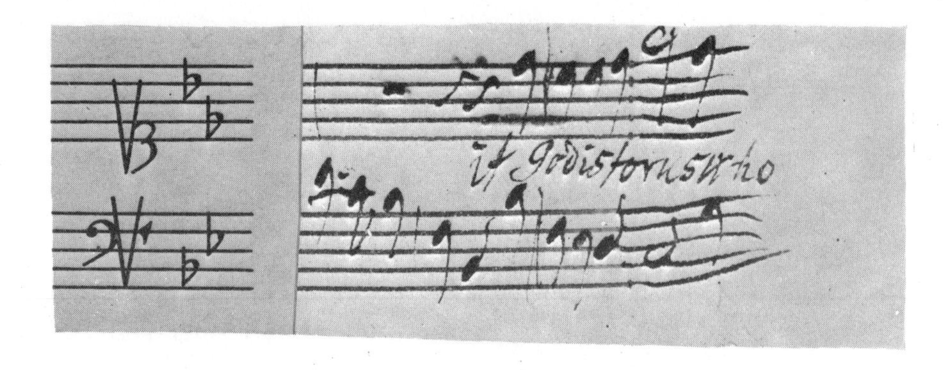

Ex. 65b

The Dublin Score has:

Ex. 66

But again observe the spread of ink where the words have been rewritten on paper roughened by a previous scraping out. Note that the second crotchet of the original is still to be seen in spite of the scraping out of the lines of the stave in the effort to remove it. And, as in bar 26, it is obvious that the additional crotchet in bar 39 was added later. These alterations were repeated by the copyist of R.M. 18 b 10, Randall and Abell, Arnold, Vincent Novello, Prout, and Chrysander in his definitive edition. But it must be said that in this instance they have the support of the Schölcher Score, a later copy by Smith. It is just possible that Smith made these alterations without consulting Handel. Certain it is that the writing in the alterations in the Dublin Score differs considerably from Handel's hand. Contrast it with the writing in the Autograph Score (See Ex. 65); note particularly the letters i and s.

This change in word arrangement clearly became general. Here it is in the Aylesford Score from Sir Newman Flower's Collection, with some obvious and untidy alterations.

Ex. 67

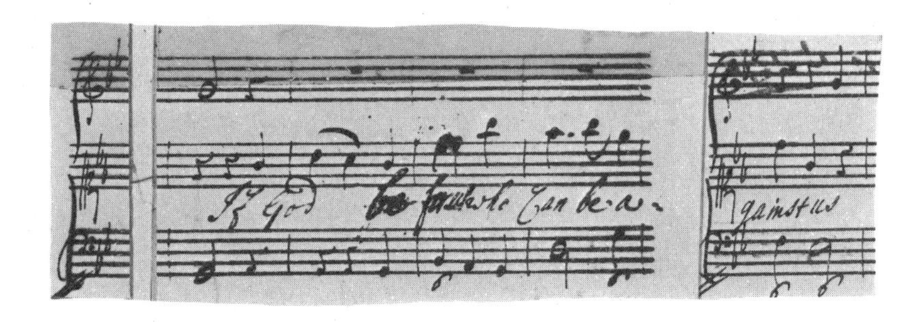

Ex. 68

The alterations completely change the character of the melody. The purposeful declamatory tread of the crotchets in bars 26 and 38 is essential to the thought. It is wrong to sacrifice this for what is, after all, a very questionable gain in balancing the verbal stress. I suggest, that what Handel wanted sung was what he wrote in the voice part of the Autograph, and this is supported by the violin part of the introduction—note the minim in bar 3:

Ex. 69

The would-be improver left this untouched, because words were not involved.

'I know that my Redeemer liveth' has suffered perhaps more than any other part of the oratorio from misguided attempts to correct Handel's 'faulty accentuation'. It is unlikely that, previous to the performance of my reconstruction first given in St Paul's Cathedral on 18th March, 1950, bars 43–45 were ever heard in any other word-arrangement than:

Ex. 70

Indeed, it is probable that they have been sung in this arrangement for 175 years, for this editing appears in the MSS Scores R.M. 18 b 10 and R.M. 18 e 2, in *Songs in Messiah* (1749) and the Randall and Abell Full Score (1767).

Yet in the Autograph Handel wrote:

Ex. 71

Ex. 72

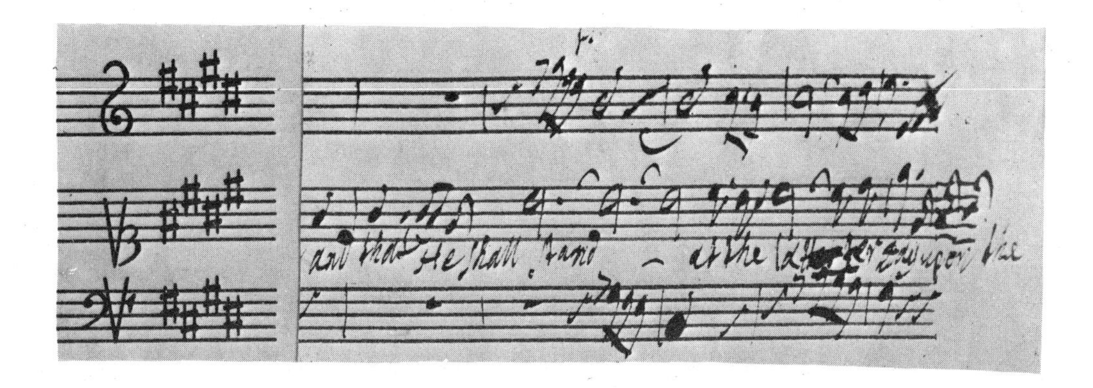

This was copied by Smith in the Dublin Score and again, later, in the Schölcher Score. It might be argued that the alteration in the 'Smith' Score (R.M. 18 b 10) was made with Handel's consent, since it appeared during his lifetime in the first printed music from *Messiah.* At first sight this seems reasonable. But the unedited version appears in three well-authenticated manuscripts—the Autograph R.M. 20 f 2 in Handel's own hand; the Dublin Score used by Handel for the first performance, (a genuine Smith Score), and the Schölcher Score made much later and also in Smith's hand.

The purpose of the 'improvement'—to remove the stress from 'that' in bar 44—is almost pointless. It is immaterial whether 'He' or 'that' is sung on the first beat of this bar, for no musicianly performer, vocal or instrumental, accents the first beat of *every* bar. He thinks in phrases, not bars. To him accent or stress is horizontal, not vertical. The natural approach in setting these words is to stress belief first in the Resurrection by means of the word 'liveth', and then in the everlasting life by placing 'shall' by itself on the last quaver, giving colour not only to 'stand' but also to 'shall'. Note how clearly Handel separated and contrasted the word 'shall' and its single quaver by connecting the two previous quavers by both horizontal tail and slur. The 'improved' version completely defeats Handel's intention—smoothing out the rhythmic leap of Handel's word-placing by slurring 'shall' over the three final quavers.

Another instance is to be found in bars 57–60. Here Handel intended:

Ex. 73

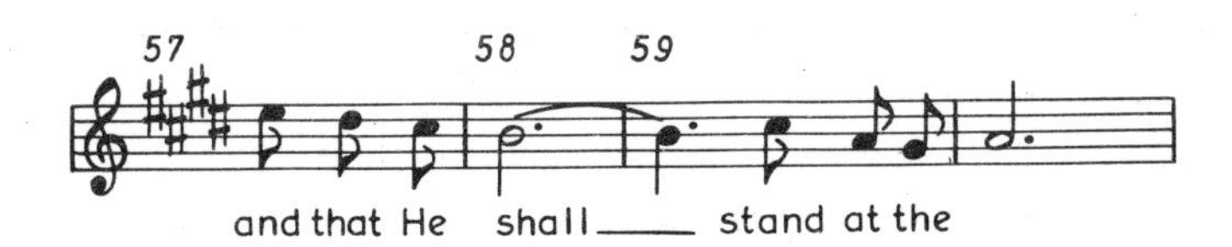

Here it is as he wrote it in the Autograph Score:

Ex. 74a

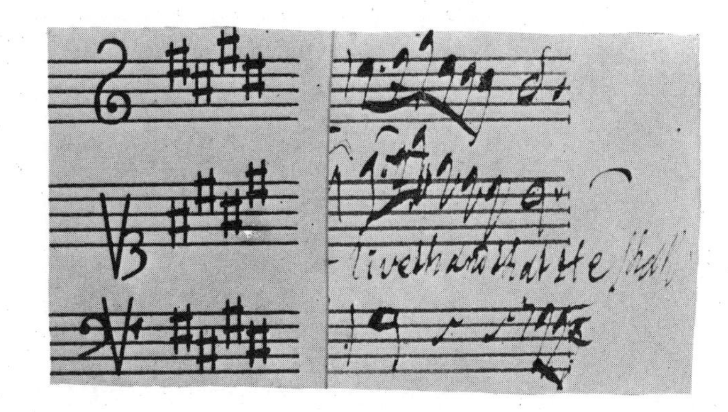

Ex. 74b

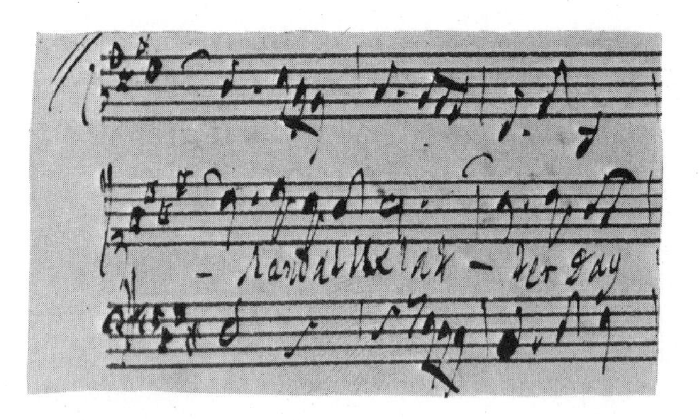

Part a of the above example occurs at the end of a stave, the words over-running the music-lines into the margin; part b is the beginning of a new stave and makes it clear beyond question that Handel intended 'shall' to be sung to the dotted minim and its tied note. Compare the stress upon 'shall' in 'He shall feed His flock':

Ex. 75

He shall_ feed his flock

The Dublin and Schölcher Scores, and also the Granville, repeat the original. But, as in the previous cases, 'improvers' began to 'edit', and produced this:

Ex. 76

And *Songs in Messiah* and the Randall and Abell Score reproduced the 'improved' version, to be followed once again by Arnold and later editors.

It has been stated that the Goldschmidt Score contains word alterations to this Air in Handel's own hand. Unfortunately I have not been able to examine this Score. As I have written elsewhere, before I could do so it was bought from the Rosenbach catalogue by a New York bookseller on behalf of a client who imposed a bond of secrecy. In the Dublin Score, however, between the pages of this Air there is a loose sheet of paper containing several alterations on which is written:

'different reading in Mr. Goldschmidt's Score from that of Sir Frederick Gore-Ouseley's.'

Part III Air 'I know that my Redeemer liveth' bars 57 and 58.

Ex. 77

and at the bottom of the sheet:

'All these alterations in adapting the words are in the same writer's hand as that of the Score.'

If this statement is correct then the alterations were certainly not in Handel's hand, for, apart from anything else, he was far too busy composing and performing to spend time in making a clean copy of any full score. It will have been observed that succeeding editors copied the altered word arrangement of Ex. 74—except, on this occasion, Prout. He preferred the Goldschmidt arrangement, in truth a much better one which, but for smoothing out the three separate quavers of bar 59, reproduces the syllabic-rhythm of the original. The repetition of the note b' to the words 'He shall stand' in *Songs in Messiah* is both banal and a travesty of Handel's rhythmic line. If we must sacrifice either the generally accepted word-stress or Handel's syllabic-rhythm, then we must sacrifice the former and retain the latter.

The loose sheet in the Dublin Score also contains a reference to bars 127–128. In the Autograph these bars appear so:

Ex. 78

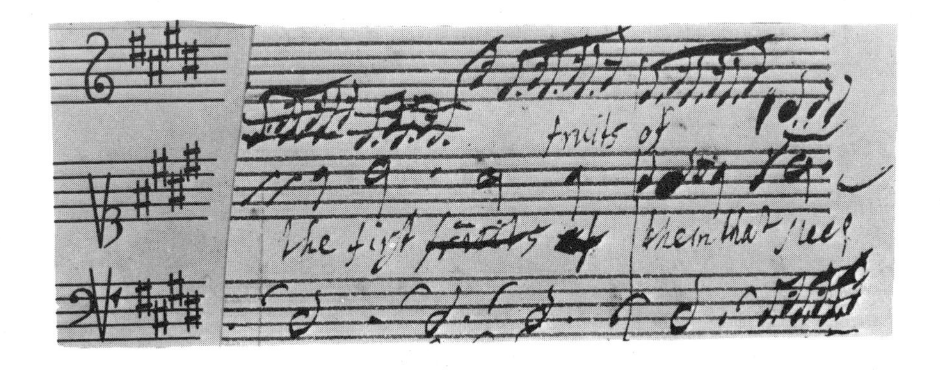

It will be seen that Handel first gave the words 'fruits of' to the minim and crotchet of bar 127, as in Ex. 79; also that the second crotchet in the next bar, from its size and nearness to the bar line, was at first a minim, making Handel's first thought:

Ex. 79

He then thought better of it, and, crossing out the words 'fruits of', wrote 'fruits' above the crotchet note a' and 'of' over the beginning of the next bar, squeezing-in a crotchet g' for this word and then filling-in the minim head to make three crotchets in the bar. This was clearly interpreted by Smith in the Dublin and Schölcher Scores as:

Ex. 80

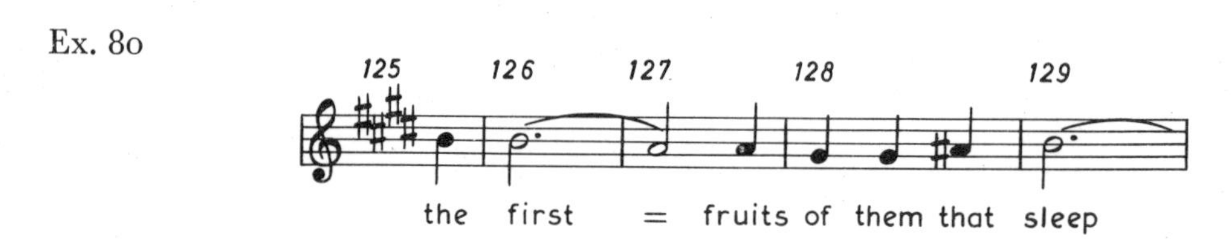


Note both the slur and the double-dash word-extension sign in bars 126 and 127.

Yet *Songs in Messiah*, Randall and Abell, Arnold, Clarke-Whitfeld, Vincent Novello and Prout (among others), carefully retain what Handel carefully discarded, as did the copyist of R.M. 18 b 10 and R.M. 18 e 2:

Ex. 81

The reference to these bars on the loose leaf in the Dublin Score is interesting, as it indicates that the Goldschmidt copy, as first written, agreed with the Dublin and Hamburg Scores; but gives what was Handel's *first* thought as one of the *corrections* (!) 'in the same writer's hand as that of the Score'.

A close examination of the Autograph—see Ex. 78—suggests that Handel's 'first thought' of this passage was itself a correction of a previous thought, arrested before it was completed. It will be observed that over the word 'that' is an ink smudge. Closer examination shows that this was a crotchet note, g' and not a' sharp. It seems, then, that Handel first intended the melody here to be:

Ex. 82

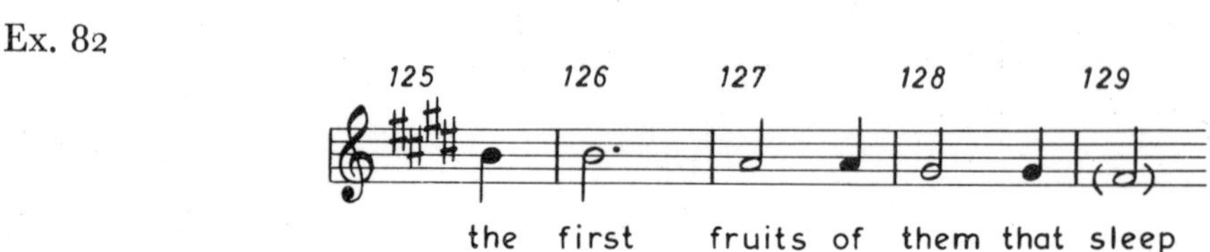

though he stopped before writing the note f'. Probably disliking the repetition of the minim-crotchet time-group, he broke the minim of bar 128 into two crotchets and altered both the direction of the melody and the word distribution. So, if we look at Exs. 82, 81, and 80, in this order, we see the mind of Handel at work. If we regard accent horizontally rather than vertically, thinking of *line* rather than of bar line, we shall not be worried by the word 'of' at the beginning of bar 128 in Handel's third thought (Ex. 80); rather shall we relish the quiet, easy movement of the three crotchets, the desire for which probably caused Handel to make the final alteration.

A similar case is to be found in bar 133–137. Here they are from the Autograph:

Ex. 83

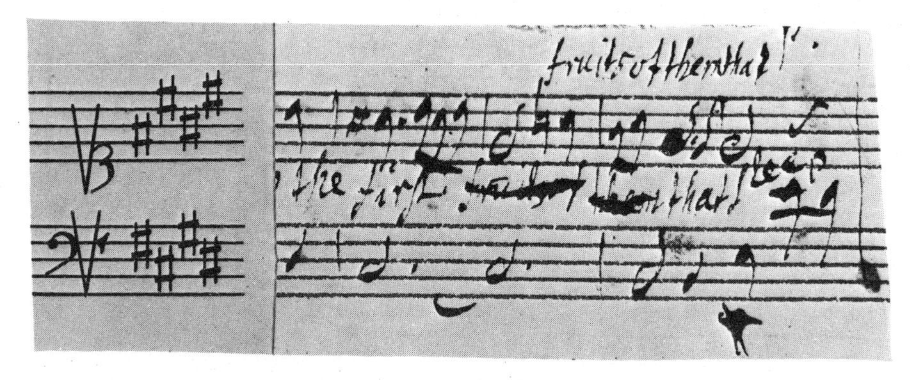

The words below the stave show Handel's first thought. The last note in bar 136 (the quaver) is part of his second thought. This bar first consisted of the two quavers followed by a minim—for the third note in the bar was obviously a minim head later filled in. Remembering his previous experience with bars 127–8, Handel again ran his pen through 'fruits of' below the stave in bar 135, and rewriting 'fruits' over the last crotchet in that bar found that he needed another note in the following bar for the word 'that', so after filling in the minim and dotting it he added the quaver.

Smith, when copying this in the Dublin Score, failed to transcribe bar 135 accurately. He would seem to have begun to copy Handel's first thought:

Ex. 84

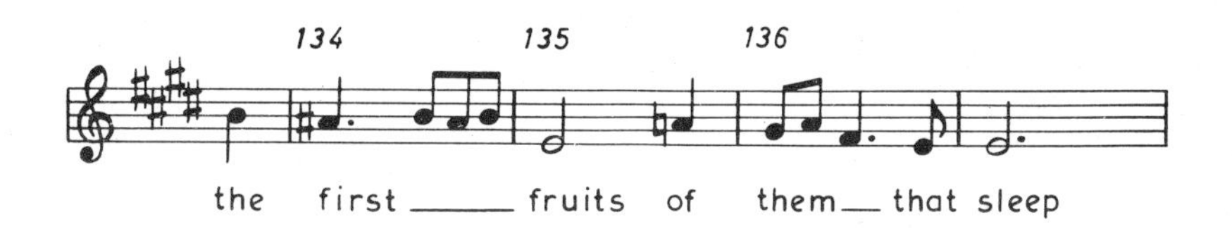


But later, when copying the Hamburg Score, he made Handel's intentions abundantly clear, not only by exact word-placing but also by the double continuation-dash under the minim:

Ex. 85

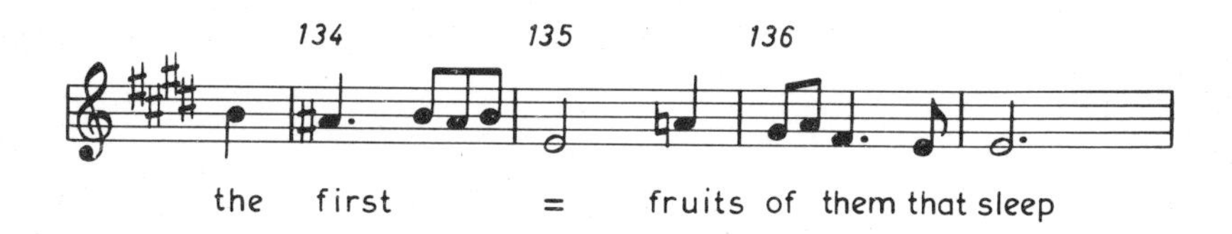

But R.M. 18 b 10 and R.M. 18 e 2 copied Handel's rejected first thought. By the time I found this I began to wonder if the copyist of R.M. 18 b 10 had copied the MSS before Handel had made these alterations. But this could not be; first because many of the alterations were obviously made by Handel at the time of composition; and secondly because in this particular case the copyist of R.M. 18 copied the altered quaver in bar 136—an alteration which arose from Handel's previous alteration in bar 135 which the copyist of R.M. 18 ignored. (This copy has now been dated as 1760.) Once again Handel's rejected first thought was copied in *Songs in Messiah*, Randall and Abell, Arnold, and later editions including Prout.

Among singers there has been much argument as to the word-placing in bars 150 and 151* of the final vocal cadence. Handel made his intention quite clear:

Ex. 86

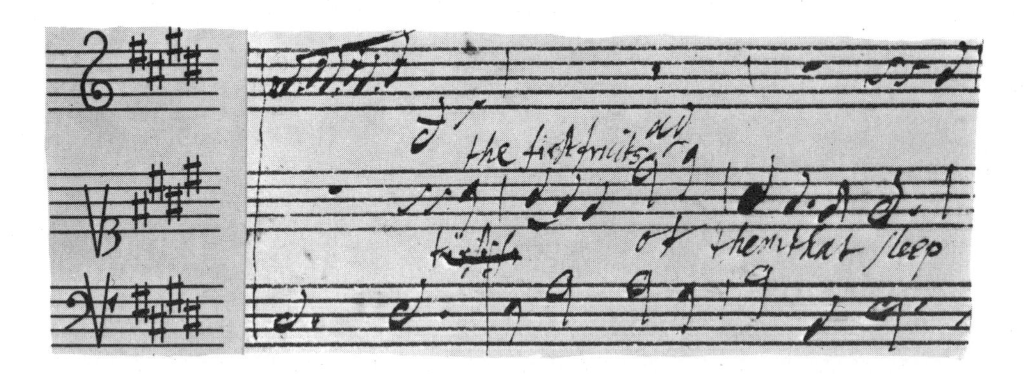


Bar 152 is somewhat ambiguous; there are three notes for only two syllables with no definite indication which two notes are to be slurred. But we will return to this. Observe for the moment Handel's determination to have 'fruits' on the last crotchet of the bar, with 'of' beginning the following bar. Even though this results (as in the two previous cases) in placing 'of' on the first beat of the next bar and in addition extending it over three beats, it does not jar. It is both singable and effective, for the 'short o' vowel is vocally very open; on it the voice rides the phrase most easily and gives expression to Handel's curving line.

Now let us consider bar 152. Handel's habit of anticipating the tonic at the end of the first of the two cadence bars, using it as a *nachschlag* or gracenote to the preceding note, suggests to us that his final intention was:

Ex. 87

But the Dublin Score gives:

Ex. 88

*The letters over bar 151 are an abbreviation for *Adagio.*

Can it be that Handel was over-ruled by Smith, or did Smith think he knew better and make the alteration without consulting Handel? Smith wrote it similarly in the Schölcher Score and in the Granville Score. It is the same in R.M. 18 b 10 and R.M. 18 e 2, and again in *Songs in Messiah*, Randall and Abell, Arnold, Clarke-Whitfeld and Vincent Novello; but not in Prout. The loose single sheet in the Dublin Score included the following among its alterations in word-arrangements in the Goldschmidt copy:

Ex. 89

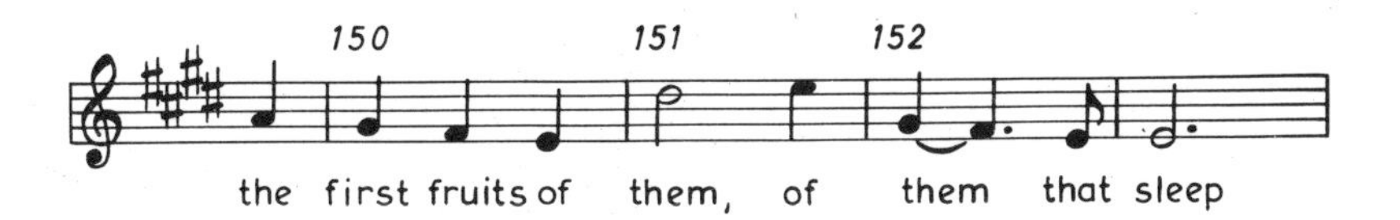


and this was reproduced by Prout.

Of all the attempts to alter Handel's word arrangements Sir Newman Flower's Aylesford Score contains quite the most astonishing:

Ex. 90

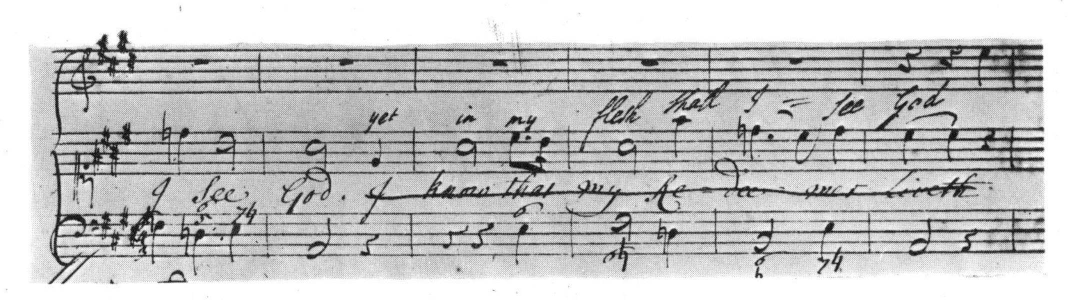


Who would think that the melody that Handel so definitely associated, in bars 111–115, with the line 'I know that my Redeemer liveth' could be sung to any other words!

# Care for Detail

AMAZEMENT at the speed at which Handel worked when composing *Messiah* has fostered the belief that he left the score unfinished, that the arias were only sketched in, and that the orchestration as it stands in the Autograph is incomplete. Anyone with a knowledge of eighteenth-century conventions and an understanding of the part played by the keyboard continuo in the orchestra of the period knows how ill-founded is such a belief; the score of *Messiah* as Handel left it is complete.

The many major after-thoughts that I have already disclosed are evidence not of carelessness but of great care. And his concern for lesser things, for the odd note, time-value or rest to be dealt with in the following cases, should prove beyond question that, in spite of the speed at which he worked, Handel still had time to attend to all essential and even some less-than-essential details.

### Just One Note

He could well be forgiven had he overlooked a slip of the pen in course of writing a *division* consisting of thirty-two semiquavers. However, the following facsimile from the chorus 'And He shall purify' beginning bar 15 shows that he detected his error in writing in the soprano just one semiquaver, the seventh, as $e''$ instead of $c''$.

Ex. 91

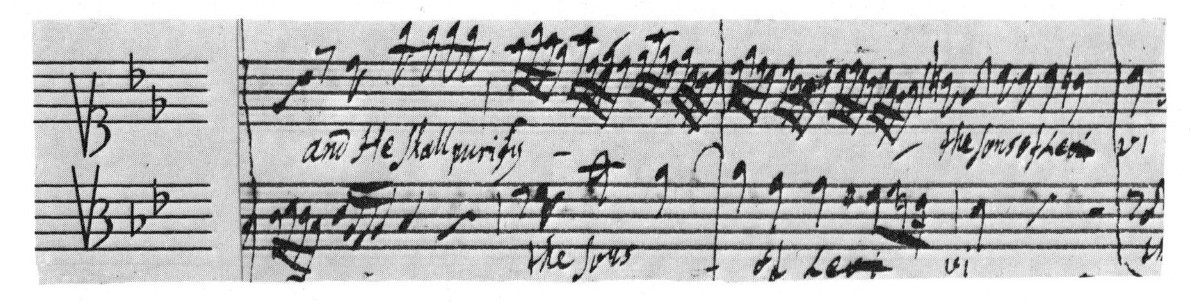


In the choral bass in bars 38 and 39 of 'Worthy is the Lamb' he wrote an excellent vocal shape, a shape with which any composer could well be satisfied.

Ex. 92

But not Handel. He obviously spent time weighing up the relative values of melodic-contour and a solidly-based harmony: he finally decided to sacrifice melodic contour, for he altered the c sharp to a.

Ex. 93

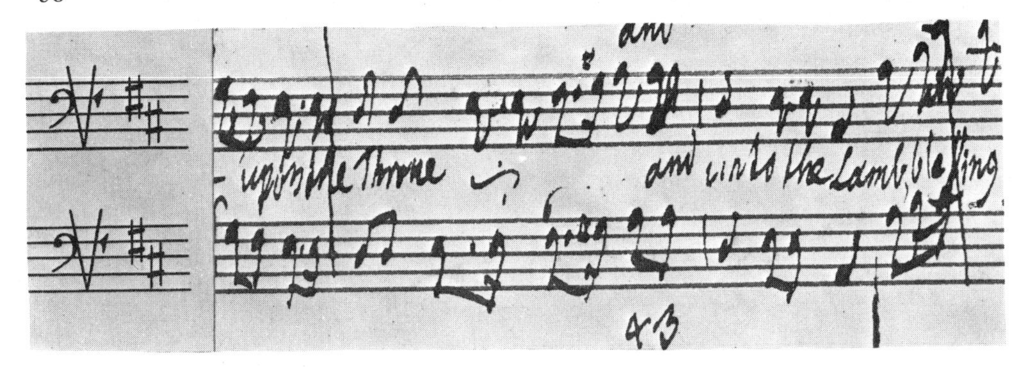

His care for detail when composing at great speed is nowhere more evident than in bar 22 of 'The Lord gave the word'. His first thought for the tenor on beat two was the note f''. This note is unexceptionable in the context. The choral harmony is strong, being well spaced as a triad in close position, with the root reinforced at the octave below. But Handel saw that the alteration of just one note would improve the line for the tenor, and give variety to the whole so he altered the second beat f'' to c''.

Ex. 94

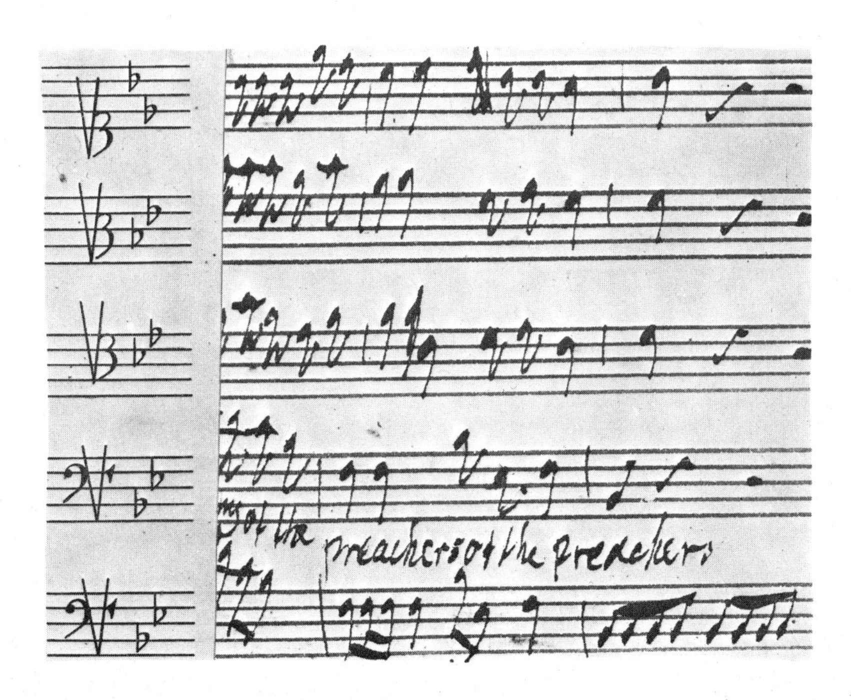

In bar 7 of 'Worthy is the Lamb' he first wrote the final three quavers in the soprano as f'' sharp.

Ex. 95

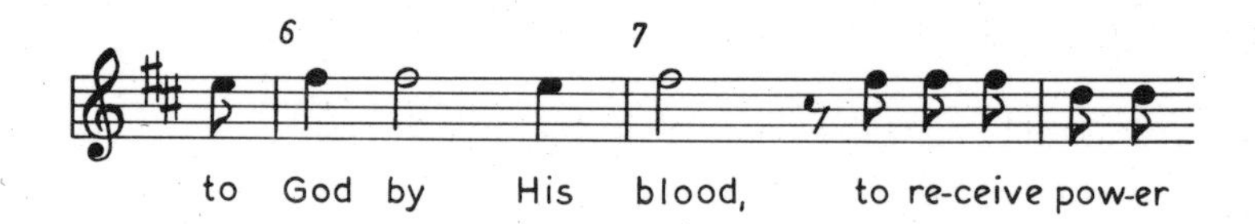


He considered sufficiently long to realise that the phrase would progress nowhere unless it started at a lower pitch.

Ex. 96

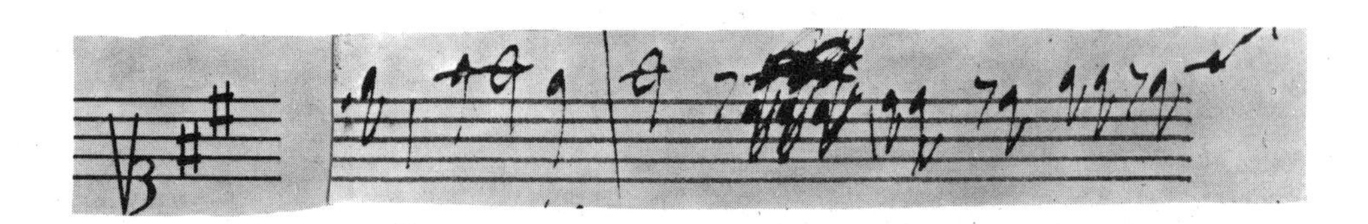

In the same passage he first wrote the two quavers in the choral bass in bar 9 beat 1 at the same pitch.

Ex. 97

He soon saw that the quaver rest on beat two of the bar had robbed him of the effect of his beloved octave leap (a veritable fingerprint, e.g. the choral bass bar 11), so he altered just one note, writing the second quaver an octave lower.

Ex. 98a

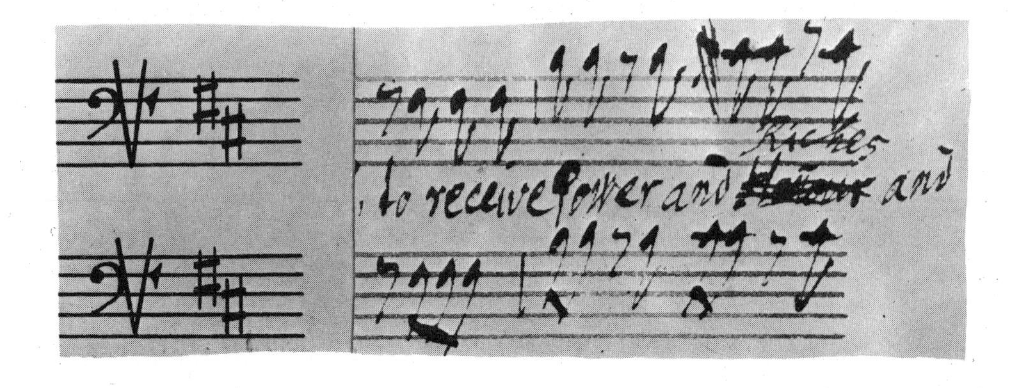

Ex. 98b

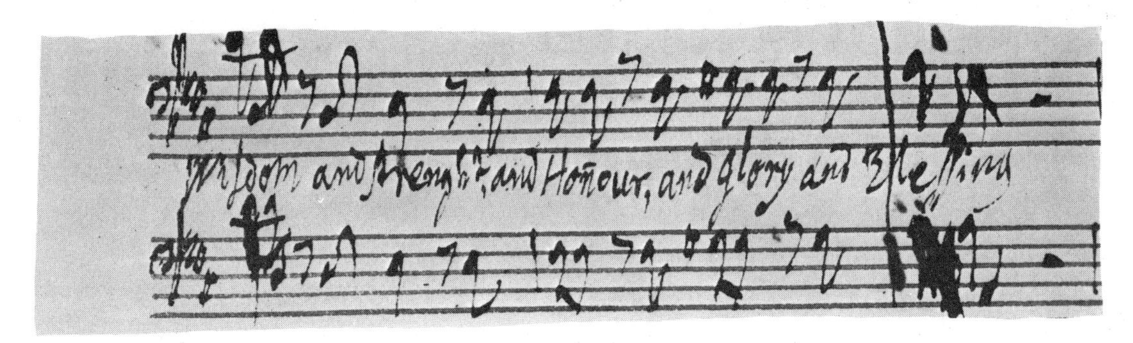

It is interesting here to note how, years later, some editors robbed him of his octave leap, but in the reverse direction. In the bass of 'Worthy is the Lamb' bar 57 Handel wrote:

Ex. 99

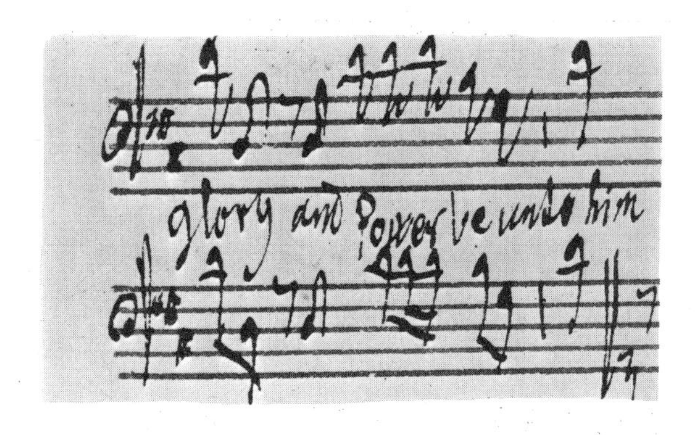


But Prout and later editors printed it:

Ex. 100

They took all power from 'power' by anticipating the leger line d on the previous quaver. Again in 'Worthy' in the soprano part bar 22 Handel first wrote the last quaver in the bar as e''.

Ex. 101

His hearing eye, however, was soon aware that the f'' sharp in bar 23 would have greater significance if approached by leap. So again he altered just one note, and with what effect!

Ex. 102

**Crotchet or Quaver ?**

Handel had time to care about the exact duration of a single note even when it did not affect the time relationship between any of the notes in the passage. In the following example from 'Thus saith the Lord' it will be seen that he first thought of the note for the word 'sea' as a quaver. Thinking further, he drew a thick crotchet stem through the quaver hook and scribbled out the following quaver rest.

Ex. 103

He first thought of bar 111 in the voice part of 'But who may abide' as:

Ex. 104

Note in the following facsimile of the Autograph in the Dublin Score the quaver hook so obviously added to the crotchet stem of the first note (compare it with the continuous stem and hook of the second note in the bar as he first wrote it). Note also the crotchet stem drawn through the quaver hook of the second note, and the crossed out quaver b flat in the *basso continuo* stave.

Ex. 105

After making the alteration, by which he so definitely reversed the previous crotchet-quaver relationship, he obviously forgot to remove the pause, for a pause over the first note would completely nullify the time relationship of short-long that he sought in making the alteration.

### Melodic versus Harmonic Interest

In 'Worthy is the Lamb', this time in an inner part—the tenor, bars 21 and 22—he altered just two notes. He first wrote:

Ex. 106

It would seem that he then decided to give greater harmonic bite to the first chord in bar 22 (by changing it from a passing 7 6 over the first inversion of G major harmony to a secondary seventh on B): he accomplished this by altering the first quaver d'' in the tenor to f'' sharp. Then, in order to avoid the unnecessary consecutive perfect fifths between the tenor and the bass, he altered the last quaver in the tenor in bar 21 from e'' to f''.

Ex. 107

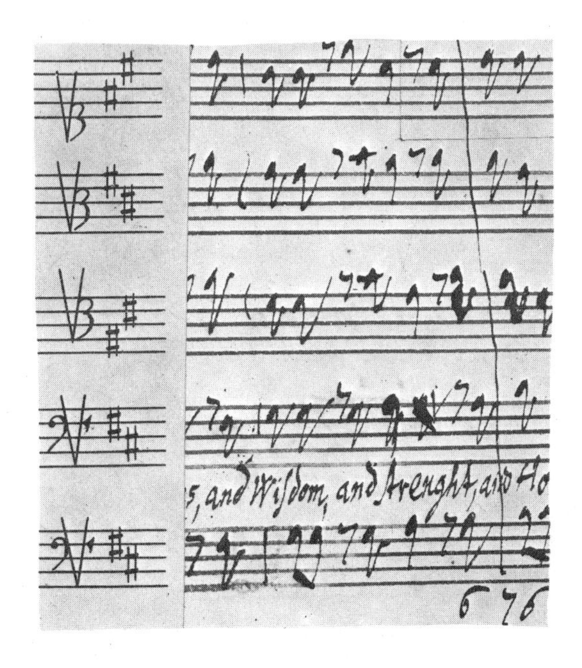

The soprano line in bar 52, still in 'Worthy', gave him much thought for he was satisfied with it only at the third attempt. It would appear that he first wrote the last two beats in bar 52 as four repeated quaver notes, c'' sharp.

Ex. 108

Then seeking variety he altered the second and fourth of those quavers.

Ex. 109

Finally, thumbing-out the fourth quaver e'' he crushed the two semi-quavers b' and a' in its place.

Ex. 110

Ex. 111

Yet again in 'Worthy', this time in the alto part, bar 63 last quaver to bar 67, he first wrote:

Ex. 112

He then altered the two quavers f' sharp in bar 64 to four semi-quavers: he evidently made the alteration immediately for there is no trace of the rest that his first thought would make necessary on the third quaver of the bar. He further decided to forego the characteristic ascending leap of a fourth across the bar line of bars 65 and 66 and between the fourth quaver and the first semi-quaver in bar 66, replacing the c' and f' sharp with the note a' in each case—thus reducing the melodic interest but strengthening the harmony.

Ex. 113

He effected a similar alteration, but in reverse, in 'All we like sheep'. In the choral bass, bars 69 and 70, he first wrote:

Ex. 114

He then improved the melodic contour by altering just two notes:

Ex. 115

Handel frequently gave greater importance to a bass theme by adding the tenor in unison, or vice versa. This he did in the passage between bars 51 and 57 in 'And the glory'. But he changed his mind about bars 56 and 57, improved the tenor line by substituting f'' sharp for b' on the first beat of bar 56 and, of even more importance, by the same act strengthened the choral harmony, thus turning a passing 7 6 over a $^{6}_{3}$ harmony into a $^{7}_{5}$ (as he later did in bar

22 of 'Worthy is the Lamb'—see Ex. 106).

Ex. 116

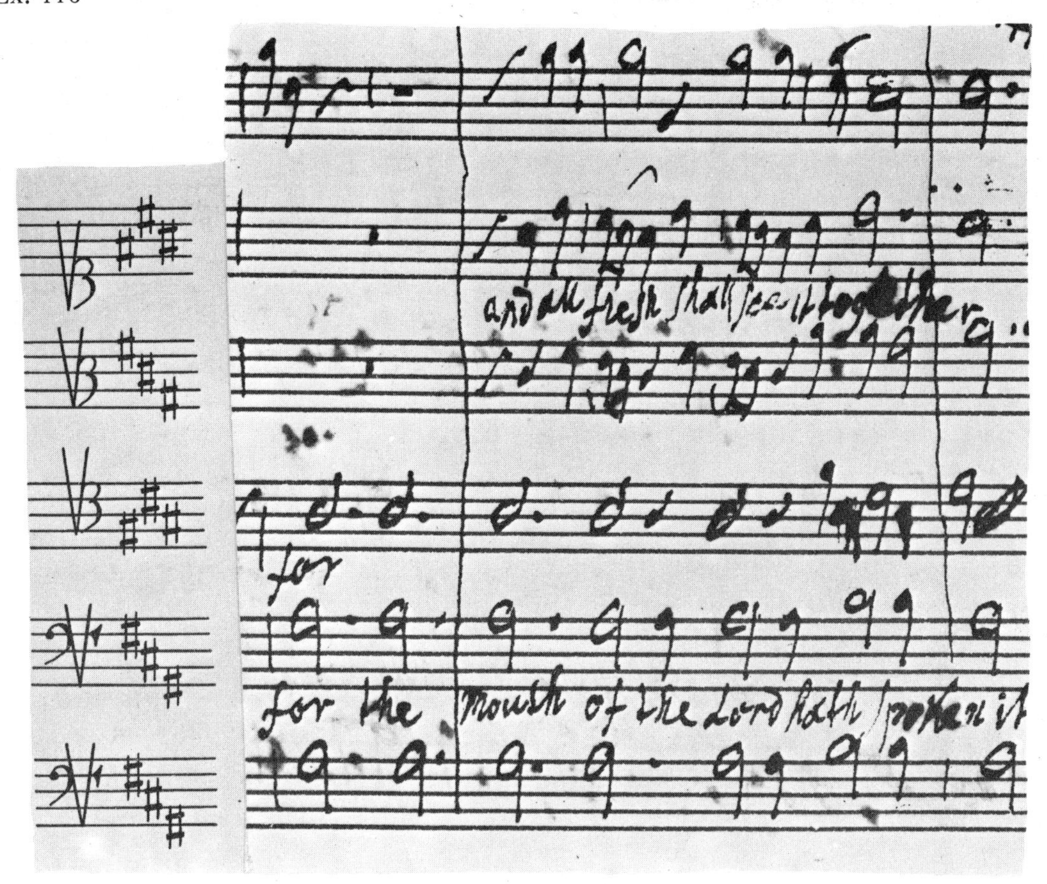


**Deletions**

Sometimes the mere mechanics of composition got the better of him and caused him to write too much. Generally, he quickly realised his mistake and crossed out the offending extension or sequence.

Who would imagine that the opening soprano *division* in 'For unto us a Child is born' was ever different from what we now sing? It was longer by some eight notes. As he first thought it, it ran straight into the following alto statement of the subject:

Ex. 117

The quaver rest in all voices on the first half of the fourth beat in bar 52 of 'All we like sheep' seems inevitable at this point, not only as a preparation for the following restatement of the *motif* but also as a momentary relief from the ever-flowing sound. Here is the passage as we know it:

Ex. 118

And here is what he first wrote:

Ex. 119

THE MARKET SQUARE IN HALLE, HANDEL'S BIRTHPLACE,
SHOWING THE TWIN TOWERS OF THE LIEBFRAUEN-KIRCHE.
THE CANTOR OF THIS CHURCH, FREDERICH WILHELM ZACHOW,
GAVE HANDEL HIS GROUNDING IN MUSIC

PHOTOKINO–KRUTGEN. HALLE (FAALE)

Ex. 120

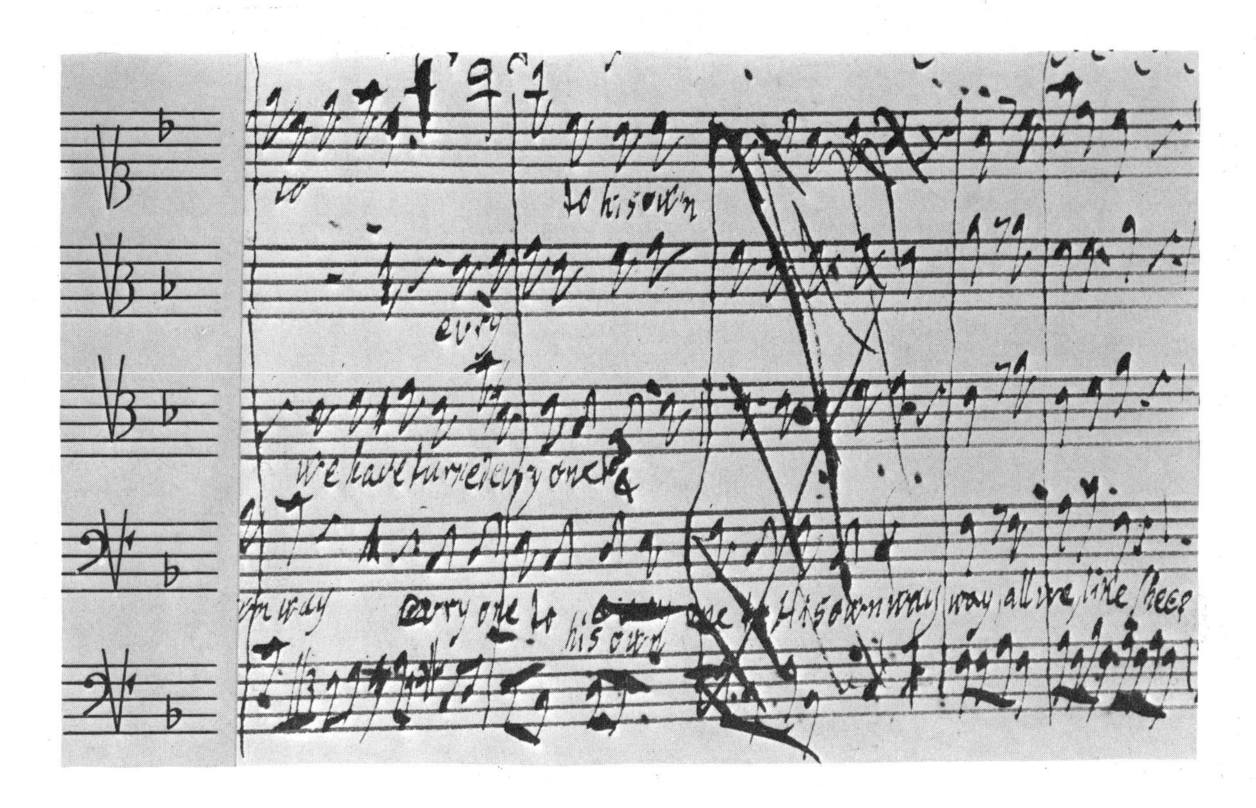


When writing the sequential *division* beginning in bar 85 of 'O thou that tellest' Handel first intended to carry the sequence to the end of the bar 87:

Ex. 121

However, he thought better of it and broke the sequence in the second half of bar 87:

Ex. 122

Ex. 123

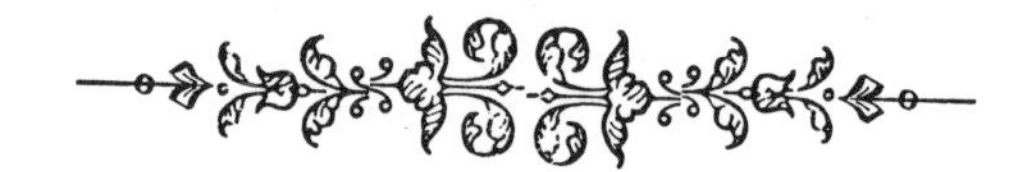

# *Practical Considerations*

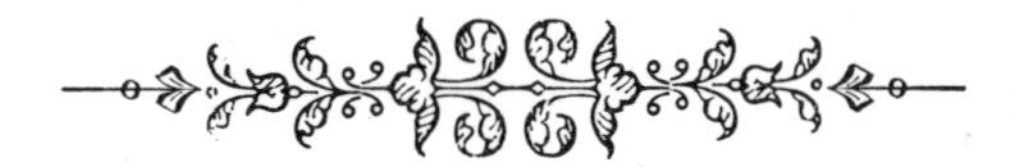

HANDEL'S second thought was often the result of practical considerations, such, for example, as the effective limits of the vocal compass. The score affords much evidence that he did not lose sight of this consideration. If in writing a point-of-imitation in the alto part he saw that the theme involved a characteristic upward leap to a note above c'' (the general upward limit for male altos, normally used in the period), almost invariably he would write the note both at the upper and lower octave, showing his preference for the upper note but also his willingness to accept the lower if the upper presented any difficulty. Here is an example from the chorus 'And with His stripes' bars 69–73.

Ex. 124

In the choral fugue 'He trusted in God' the polyphonic development led to the *subject* beginning in the soprano on the high g''; this, if the original subject was repeated exactly, involved a high c''' on the first quaver in bar 53.

Ex. 125

One can imagine the regret with which he substituted for this c''' a repetition of the note g'', for this involved the loss of the derisory colour of the upward leap on the second syllable of the word 'deliver'. He was not, however, to be completely foiled for, although normally he did not trouble to fill in the orchestral parts in a choral fugue where the instruments merely doubled the voices, in this case he wrote in the first violin stave just these notes in order to include the high c'''.

Ex. 126

Of the many such instances a striking example is that in bars 42 and 43 of the soprano part in 'Worthy is the Lamb'. It will be seen that he first thought of this figure an octave higher beginning on the soprano high a''. He would seem to have wanted the soprano imitation of the previous alto figure to be at the octave above for greater contrast. His spirit was willing, but he feared that the soprano vocal flesh would be weak.

Ex. 127

Observe the dot after the bar line—a method of showing the tied note across the bar line.

Obviously he hankered after that soprano high a'' for in bar 29 of the soprano part in the

'Hallelujah' he wrote:

Ex. 128

It is clear that his first intention was that the soprano should give a more or less identical answer to the bass figure that began with the last two semiquavers in bar 27. True, at the beginning of the bar 29 he wrote only a note head (a method he used for showing a preference for the upper note if it could be sung); but in the second half of the bar he got as far as drawing the stem and semiquaver hooks. Observe the hooks obscured by the superimposed note head.

**Syllabic-Rhythm**

Elsewhere I have written of Handel's syllabic-rhythm. There is an excellent example, not in a solo but in a choral part, and an inner part at that, so greatly did he care. It is in bars 70 and 71 of the tenor part in the 'Hallelujah'. His first thought was:

Ex. 129

It is fairly clear from the style of the alteration that, no sooner had he written the time values for the above word-distribution, than, disliking the result, he altered the words solely in order to obtain a more conclusive rhythm.

Ex. 130

Ex. 131

Note (1) the crotchet stem drawn through the quaver hook of the first quaver G sharp
(2) the complete crossing out of the second quaver G sharp to the word 'and' (also the final note A)
(3) the insertion of the note for the new word 'reign' necessitated by the word alteration.

He first thought of bars 136 to 138 in 'The trumpet shall sound' as:

Ex. 132

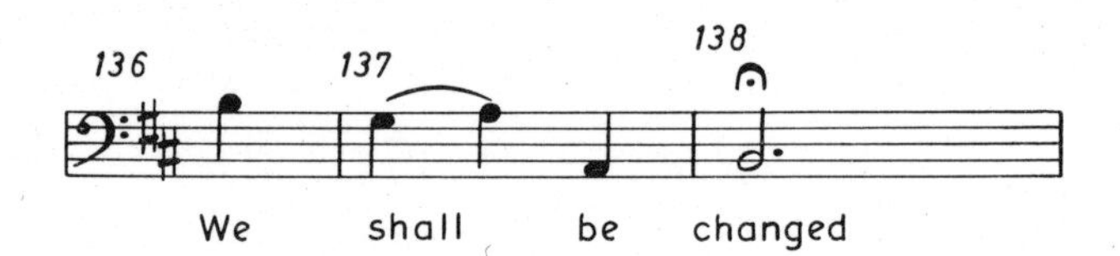


But, yet again, his feeling for syllabic-rhythm caused him to strengthen the phrase by removing the couplet slur inherent in his original word placing:

Ex. 133

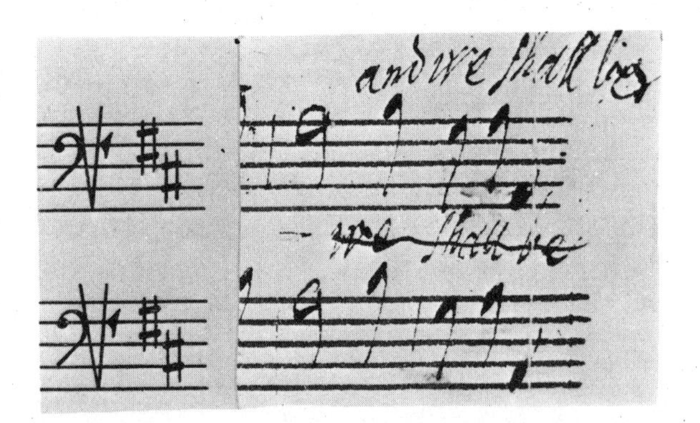

On occasion Handel's second thought became an extension of the phrase. He first thought of treating bars 82 to 84 of 'The trumpet shall sound' in a manner similar to the comparable bars 32 to 34, using the words 'And the death (sic) shall be raised' (later altered to 'the trumpet shall sound'), with the *basso continuo* of bar 83 running practically in unison with the voice.

Ex. 134

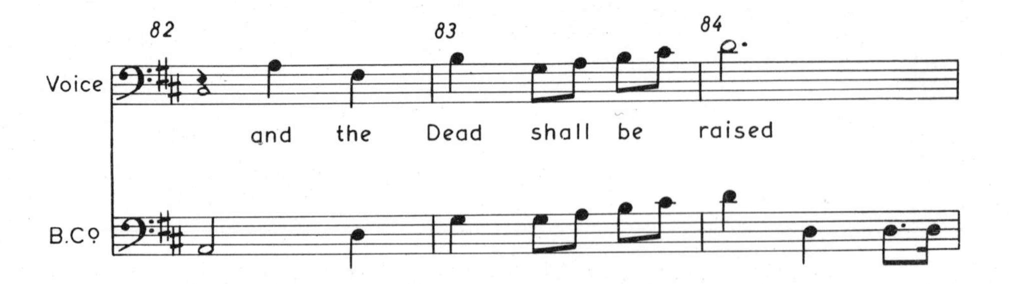


He then completed the unison in bar 83 by altering the *basso continuo* in bars 82 and 83.

Ex. 135

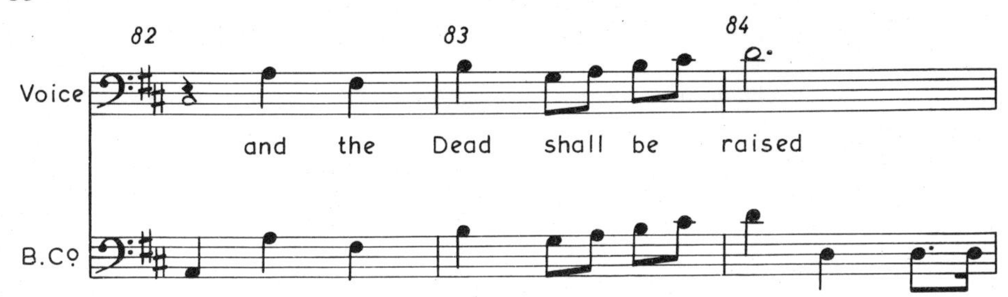


At some time he decided to alter the words and crossed through the resulting redundant note in the vocal stave in bar 82, added the now necessary second crotchet rest below the existing one and altered the *basso continuo* in bar 82.

Ex. 136

Ex. 137

It will be seen from the facsimile

(a) that the first *basso continuo* note A (bar 82), from its size, was originally a minim, later filled in as a crotchet

(b) that the vertical smudge in the *basso continuo* immediately before the note f sharp in bar 82 was originally the third beat note d'

(c) that the mark across the stem of the crossed out crotchet note b in the *basso continuo* was originally the note g on beat one of bar 83

(d) that, after inking-out his first attempt in bar 83 of the *basso continuo,* he crushed his final solution of the whole bar against the last note of the voice

(e) that the last *basso continuo* note of his first attempt, the crotchet third line a, bar 84 beat 2, is hidden in the left-hand curve of the minim (his second attempt); note its thin upward stem.

The resulting variety in structure—a four bar extension of the phrase—the independent *basso continuo* moving by contrary motion—and the emphasis arising from the repetition of the words on the ascending scale passage from g to d' in bars 87 and 88 are well worth the considerable trouble he took.

**Ornamentation**

Some of Handel's second thoughts afford an insight into his feeling for ornamentation. In the middle section of 'The trumpet shall sound' bars 181 to 184 he first wrote:

Ex. 138

He later decided to grace his own melody and altered bar 183 to read:

Ex. 139

Ex. 140

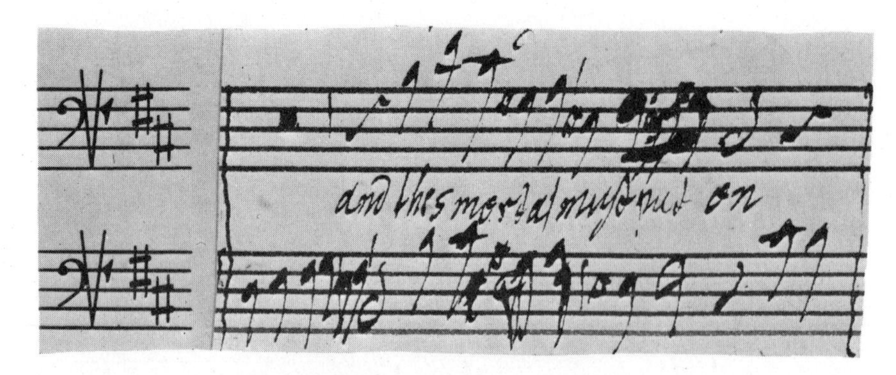

Here once again the size of the second note in the voice part in bar 183 of the facsimile indicates that originally it was a minim, the voice being in exact unison with the *basso continuo.*

An illuminating example of Handel's feeling for ornamentation and clear proof that not only did he expect but that he wanted it is the passage in 'Rejoice greatly' beginning in bar 33. In the comparable bars in the original setting in $\frac{12}{8}$ in the Autograph Score Handel wrote:

Ex. 141

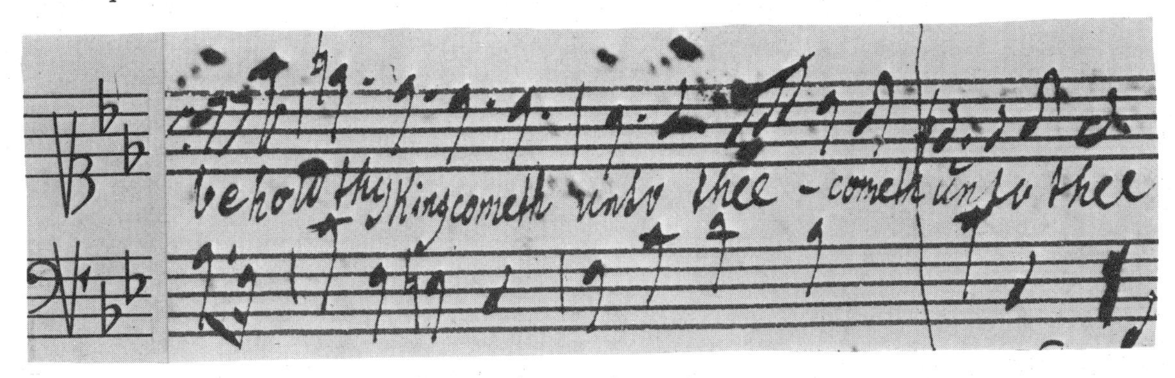


Singers were accustomed to ornamenting notes such as these. A plain descending passage of this sort was unthinkable and unsingable! Composers expected decoration; they occasionally indicated it—much to the disgust of singers, who regarded the decoration of the vocal line as their responsibility and prerogative. Tosi expresses this disgust in his *Observations on the Florid Song or Sentiments on the Ancient and Modern Singers* (written in Italian but published in an English translation in London in 1742, the year *Messiah* was first performed). 'Poor Italy!' he wrote, 'pray tell me: do not the singers now-a-days know where the appoggiaturas are to be made unless they are pointed out with the finger?' When Handel rewrote the Air in common time he most certainly pointed out the appoggiaturas with his finger! He might have been content with the simple appoggiaturas usually sung today:

Ex. 142

Since they were so printed in the Randall and Abell Full Score we may take it that they have been sung in this manner by some singers since 1767. Yet Handel did not write them so in the Autograph copy in the Dublin Score, neither have I found them so in any of the primary and principal secondary manuscripts that I have examined. Handel wanted a more elaborate ornament which he wrote in the conventional manner in the violin part in the ritornello in bar 42:

Ex. 143

Not to be confused with the trilled couplets in bars 7 and 8.

Ex. 144

But in the voice part of bars 32 to 36, to make doubly sure he wrote it out in full:

Ex. 145

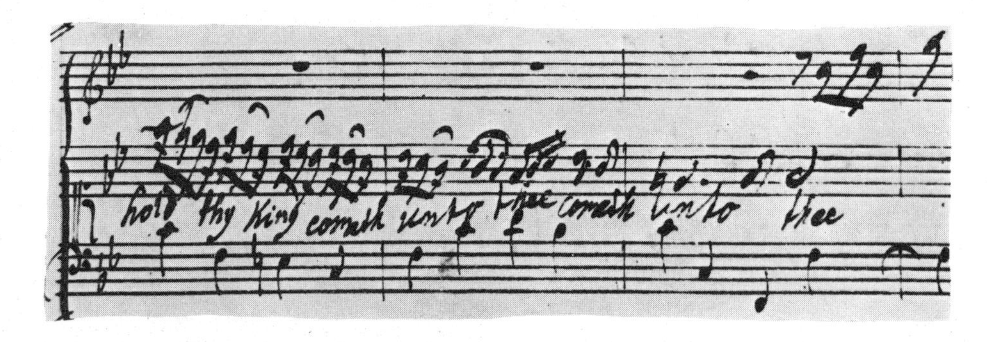


**Harmonic Progression and Melodic Design**

Handel well knew how to create tension and repose—by means of harmonic progression (whether within a movement or on a larger scale by the key-relationship between movements) and by melodic design.

His system of key-relationships between adjoining movements is a delight to analyse, he moves so easily and with such colour from movement to movement. He is especially fond of the relationship of a third—from the major to its relative minor or vice versa, to the submediant, the flattened submediant, and the mediant minor; out of the 53 numbers in *Messiah* no less than 34 stand in this relationship to the preceding one. Apart from these 34, the other movements all pass between tonic and dominant or subdominant, with the exception of a single case which moves to the supertonic—from 'He was despised' in E flat major to 'Surely He hath borne our griefs' in F minor.

Handel makes much use of recitative in moving from key to key as did all composers of the period. Only four of the sixteen recitatives end in the same key as they began in, and of these four only two remain in the same key throughout. The other twelve move through anything from two to six different keys.

His use of the chromatic modulation to the flattened submediant is most colourful: the brilliance of the F major 'Lift up your heads' following the A major 'But Thou didst not leave'; the warmth of the B flat major 'Rejoice greatly' coming after the dazzling 'mixture' quality of the D major 'Glory to God'. Perhaps his most moving use of the submediant progression is after the mocking final C minor cadence of 'He trusted in God', where the music sinks with such pathos into the chord of A flat major for the recitative 'Thy rebuke hath broken His heart'. Was ever a major chord so full of sorrow? In this instance it is a progression and not a modulation, for the real key is F minor, and truth to tell the opening A flat major chord takes on greater colour by reason of our foreknowledge of the next harmony.

This recitative is a fine example of the use of key and harmonic progression for emotional colour.

Beginning on the chord of A flat major, it sighs its way into the F minor leading-note triad, then moves through G minor and E minor, and following upon the tenor's 'Thy rebuke hath broken His heart' of bars 6 and 7 comes the lovely *tierce de Picardie** of the strings, made the more moving by the sense of the false relation (notwithstanding the intervening chord) between the G natural of the first violins in bar 6 and the G sharp of the *basso continuo* in bar 7. Progressing through A minor to D minor, Handel makes most poignant use of the chromatic chord of the flattened supertonic (E flat) in bar 11; again, moving to B minor, he uses the same chromatic harmony and ends with another *tierce de Picardie.* Although the third of the chord is not in the string parts in the Autograph, he indicates major harmony for the harpsichord by the figuring, the raised third. Incidentally, this is the most fully-figured movement in the Autograph; in 18 bars of slow-moving sustained chords Handel figured 20 harmonies.

The melody of this recitative is of equal interest. The passionate intensity created by the rising third of the first two notes is followed by the drop, with only one note intervening, to the octave below; although the following note of 'heaviness' is somewhat intensified by the repetition of the sentence at a slightly higher pitch, the first complete phrase remains at this low level. The next phrase rises from this low e' (bar 8) by three similarly shaped although not identical figures, to the high g''.

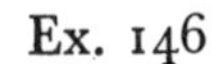
Ex. 146

After remaining for two bars around d'' the tension is reduced by the repetition of the same figure at a lower level: finally dropping a fourth at the cadence, the sorrow having surrendered its note of passion for one of resignation.

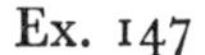
Ex. 147

It may well be said that this accompanied recitative, following upon 'He trusted in God', was intensely felt and perfectly contrived. But it was very nearly not so perfectly contrived, for the low registration of 'He is full of heaviness' was not the original intention. In the Autograph Score this bar 3 is so altered that it is impossible to see exactly what Handel's first thought was. The carbon ink will not yield to infra-red or ultra-violet radiation. But examined by means of transmitted light it would appear that he first intended a rising arpeggio.

Ex. 148

*A major cadence to music in a minor key.

There is even a reasonably clear suggestion of an unbelievable e''. It is however not possible to interpret with anything like detailed accuracy, for the difficulty is added to by several ink soaks from the other side of the paper. But certain it is that his first thoughts for these words were a rising figure. Equally certain is it that he immediately recognised that any upward curve here would ruin the emotional structure of the whole.

Ex. 149

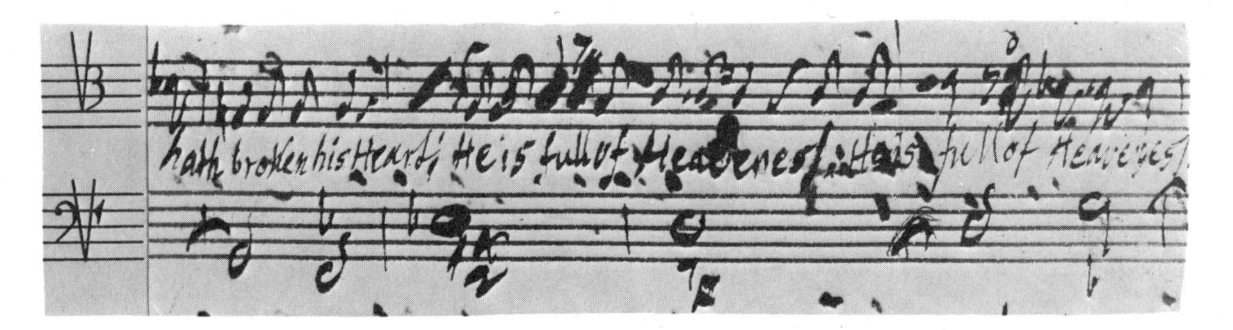

(Observe also that the second note in bar 5 was first a'. Having altered it to d'' he wrote the letter d above the alteration in order to remove any ambiguity.)
In similar case is bar 3 of 'Behold and see'. He first wrote:

Ex. 150

Had he retained this melodic line in the voice then the following short ritornello rising to g'' in the first violin would have lost its poignancy by reason of anticipation. It it reasonable to assume that when Handel arrived at the ritornello he immediately recognised this fact and effected a remarkable change by altering just two notes in the vocal line (the first two quavers of bar 3) with a consequent alteration of one note in the *basso continuo:*

Ex. 151

Ex. 152

It will be seen in passing that having altered the bass line he omitted to remove the figuring (now inaccurate) from under the note E in the *basso continuo.*

## *In Conclusion*

The examples in this book do not by any means exhaust Handel's after-thoughts in *Messiah,* but are sufficient to prove that while with him speed and carelessness are not necessarily bed-fellows inspiration and craftmanship are unquestionably so. Inspiration is not a divine ink which pours in at the head and out at the finger tips until the work is complete. It is the spark that lights the fire which craftmanship must keep aflame. As I said earlier, the artist deserves neither praise nor blame for the ideas that come to him, but only for what he does or fails to do with them. His genius lies in recognising the germ and then transforming it into a work of art.

In Handel's own manuscripts we find abundant proof that he was no hasty scribbler, but an artist and an indefatigable craftsman—in truth, a genius.

# *THE PRINCIPAL MANUSCRIPTS*

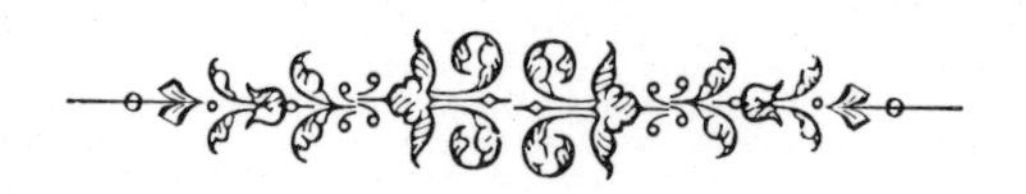

## *And Where They May Be Seen*

*THE AUTOGRAPH SCORE* is in the British Museum, London. This is the only complete score in Handel's writing. It contains all of *Messiah* as it is sung generally today, with the exception of two numbers. These two numbers, 'But who may abide' and 'Rejoice greatly', are essentially different from the known popular settings. This volume also contains in an appendix the setting of 'How beautiful are the feet' for alto duet and chorus.

*THE DUBLIN SCORE* is in the library of St Michael's College, Tenbury, Worcestershire. This was used by Handel at the first performance of the oratorio which took place in Dublin on April 13th, 1742. It was copied by Smith Senior, Handel's amanuensis. The volume is of considerable importance as it contains, in autograph, the settings popularly sung of 'But who may abide' and 'Rejoice greatly'.

*THE SCHÖLCHER SCORE* is in the Staats und Universitäts Bibliothek, Hamburg. This copy also was made by Smith Senior (with some additions in the hand of Smith Junior). It is of interest for it would appear to have been used in performance and contains 'He was despised' transposed a fifth higher for Soprano: 'He shall feed His flock' in a clean copy of the popular alto-soprano arrangement and with the names of two male singers in the top margin: in the Autograph Score Handel wrote 'He shall feed His flock' for soprano throughout.

*THE GOLDSCHMIDT SCORE* its present whereabouts is unknown. Mr Fleming, formerly associated with Dr Rosenbach, has informed me that the score was bought from the Rosenbach catalogue by a New York bookseller who sold it under a condition of secrecy.

It was in the possession of Dr Otto Goldschmidt, the musician and husband of the famous singer Jenny Lind who was the model for St Cecelia on the Handel monument in the market place in Handel's birthplace, Halle, in Eastern Germany. It is known to contain ornamentation for the Da Capo of 'He was despised', and alterations to the word arrangement in 'I know that my Redeemer liveth'.

It is a great pity that, hidden in some collection, it is not available for research.

*THE FOUNDLING SCORE* is in the Thomas Coram Foundation, London (the Foundling Hospital of Handel's day). This doubtless is the score willed by Handel to the Hospital. It would appear not to have been used and, although not in the usual presentation format, has the appearance of a presentation copy.

*THE SOLO PART BOOKS* in the Thomas Coram Foundation. They are of interest for two reasons. Firstly they appear to have been used in performance for each book bears the name of a singer: the 'Second Soprano' book—Sigra Passerini, 'Principal Alto'—Sigra Galli, 'Tenore Principale' — Mr Beard, 'Basso Principale '— Mr Wass. (Unfortunately the First Soprano book is missing: it was Handel's custom to have two soprano soloists.) Secondly they afford evidence that the soloists also sang all the choruses, for each book contains, in addition to the solos, the appropriate voice part of every chorus, with clear instructions to the soloist to, as it were, get a move on and lead his or her own voice in the choruses—such as 'Segue il Coro presto' and 'Volti presto e segue'.

*ORCHESTRAL PARTS* in the Thomas Coram Foundation. These consist of parts for violins I and II, viola, violoncello, oboe, bassoon, trumpet and timpani. It will be observed that there is no part for the double basses. We know however that two double basses played in Handel's own performances. The minute books of the Hospital contain detailed accounts for performances given in the Chapel which include the names of the orchestral players and the fees paid to them. In the accounts for the performance given on April 27th, 1758 the double bass players were Dietrich and Sworms. The orchestral parts are of interest as they show contemporary practice in relation to the use of oboes and bassoons.

*THE GRANVILLE SCORE* in the British Museum. This is in the manuscript room among the Egerton papers. It was made by Smith Senior for Handel's friend Bernard Granville of Calwick Abbey, Staffordshire. Its value lies in its early date—c 1742, and its contents—it contains the alto duet and chorus setting of 'How beautiful' and the tenor solo (arioso) setting of 'Their sound is gone out'.

*THE HARPSICHORD PART* in the British Museum. This is in the hand of Jennens who compiled the libretto of *Messiah.* It is incomplete for it finishes with 'Glory to God'. It contains copious figuring in 'The people that walked in darkness' and quite elaborate ornamentation elsewhere. Whatever Jennens may or may not have been as a musician the part is an indication of contemporary practice.

*THE MARSH LIBRARY SCORE* in the Archbishop Marsh Library, Dublin. This score is the source for the alternative setting of 'But who may abide' as a recitative.

*THE LENNARD SCORE* in the Fitzwilliam Museum, Cambridge. This contains much ornamentation, added in pencil throughout the choral parts in addition to the solos, probably in the early nineteenth century.

*THE 1742 WORD BOOK* in the British Museum. This is the word-book of the first performance of the oratorio which was given in Neal's Music Hall, Fishamble Street, Dublin on April 13th, 1742. It bears the imprint 'George Faulkner—Dublin 1742—price a British six-pence'.

The book indicates, although not completely, which of the various alternative versions were sung at the first performance. For example it proves conclusively, by means of the printed text, that 'How beautiful are the feet' was sung not in the popular G minor air setting to the text from Romans Chapter X Verses 15 and 18 but in the alto duet and chorus setting to the text from Isaiah Chapter LII Verses 7 and 9.

*THE NEWMAN FLOWER COLLECTION*

at Tarrant Keynston, Dorset. This collection is unique among other reasons in that its *Messiah* manuscripts include score, solo part books, orchestral parts (strings only) and word books. For years we have been accustomed to refer to the Foundling orchestral parts as the only known set of contemporary orchestral parts. This in future will need to be qualified by the addition of the word 'complete'.

The score is noteworthy for at least two reasons; the first—the *basso continuo* of 'The people that walked in darkness' is even more copiously figured than it is in the Jennens Harpsichord part (a clear indication that this air was neither *Tasto Solo* nor *All' Unisono* but was harmonized in eighteenth century performances); the second—that it contains a curious mis-binding. After 47 bars of the chorus 'Let us break' part of the Hallelujah is interpolated (from bar 7 beat 3 to bar 47 beat 2), after which follows the remainder of 'Let us break' from bar 48. (A point of interest—Segue is often spelt Siegue.) The word book, 'printed for J. Watts and sold by R. Dod at the Bible and Key, Ave-Mary-Lane near Stationers Hall, 1759', is of the last performance given by Handel before his death. It affords proof that in Handel's day the first section of 'Lift up your heads' was sung as a semi-chorus. There are four solo part books—Canto Primo, Alto Primo, Tenor Primo, and Basso Primo. As the Alto Primo does not contain 'He was despised', and as each of the other books at this point has 'Song Tacet', it could be that at the performance for which these part books were written it was sung by the second soprano soloist in the transposed version from the Schölcher score.

*TWO OTHER VOLUMES*

of interest to the lovers of *Messiah*, but not manuscripts, are the first printed music and the first printed Full Score. They are

*SONGS IN MESSIAH*

in the William C. Smith Collection, Chislehurst, Kent. This is a rare copy of the first edition. Later editions printed as *The* Songs in Messiah (the italics are the author's) are to be found in the British Museum and many other collections. This publication contains the air 'O Thou that tellest' in its form for counter-tenor, i.e. printed in the treble clef at the octave above.

*THE RANDALL AND ABEL FULL SCORE*

is in the British Museum as well as many other collections.

# *INDEX*

## MESSIAH



## GENERAL